Oscar Fingal O'Flahertie Wills Wilde (16 October 1854 – 30 November 1900) was an Irish poet and playwright. After writing in different forms throughout the 1880s, he became one of London's most popular playwrights in the early 1890s. He is best remembered for his epigrams and plays, his novel The Picture of Dorian Gray, and the circumstances of his criminal conviction for homosexuality, imprisonment, and early death at age 46. Wilde's parents were successful Anglo-Irish intellectuals in Dublin. Their son became fluent in French and German early in life. At university, Wilde read Greats; he proved himself to be an outstanding classicist, first at Trinity College Dublin, then at Oxford. He became known for his involvement in the rising philosophy of aestheticism, led by two of his tutors, Walter Pater and John Ruskin. After university, Wilde moved to London into fashionable cultural and social circles. (Source: Wikipedia)

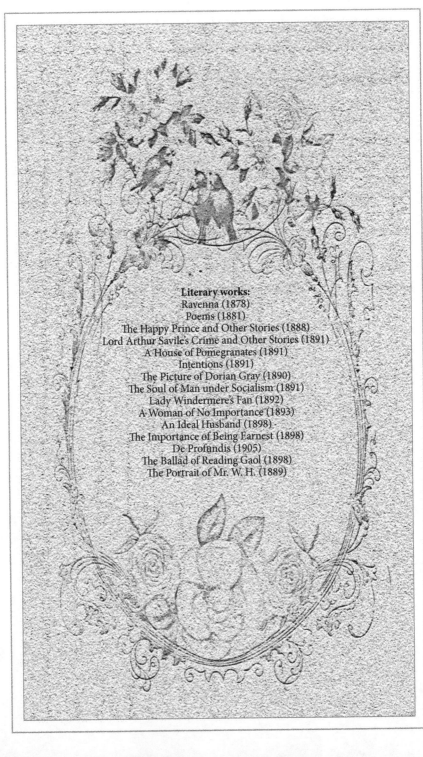

Literary works:
Ravenna (1878)
Poems (1881)
The Happy Prince and Other Stories (1888)
Lord Arthur Savile's Crime and Other Stories (1891)
A House of Pomegranates (1891)
Intentions (1891)
The Picture of Dorian Gray (1890)
The Soul of Man under Socialism (1891)
Lady Windermere's Fan (1892)
A Woman of No Importance (1893)
An Ideal Husband (1898)
The Importance of Being Earnest (1898)
De Profundis (1905)
The Ballad of Reading Gaol (1898)
The Portrait of Mr. W. H. (1889)

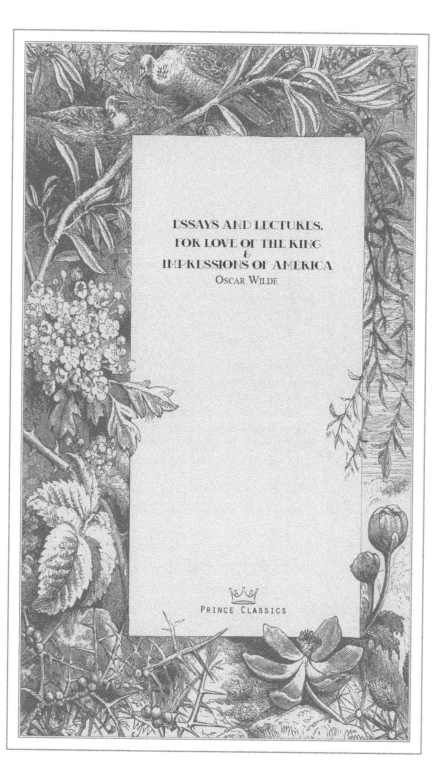

ESSAYS AND LECTURES,
FOR LOVE OF THE KING
&
IMPRESSIONS OF AMERICA

Oscar Wilde

PRINCE CLASSICS

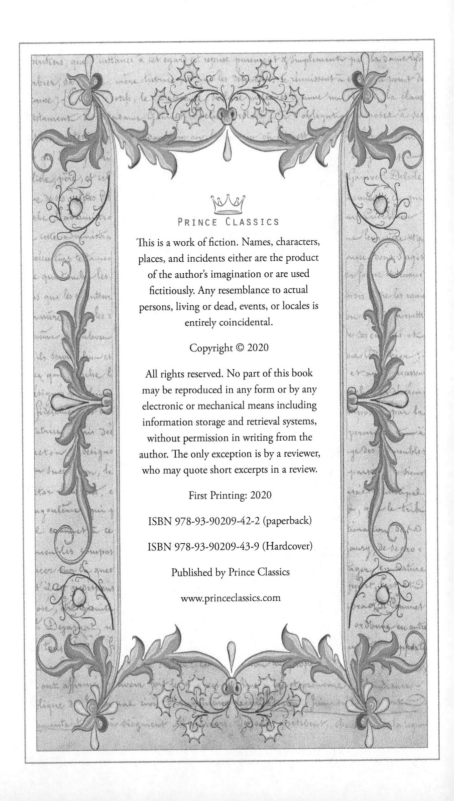

PRINCE CLASSICS

First Printing: 2020

ISBN 978-93-90209-42-2 (paperback)

ISBN 978-93-90209-43-9 (Hardcover)

Published by Prince Classics

www.princeclassics.com

Contents

ESSAYS AND LECTURES,
FOR LOVE OF THE KING
&
IMPRESSIONS OF AMERICA

ESSAYS AND LECTURES

PREFACE

With the exception of the *Poems in Prose* this volume does not contain anything which the author ever contemplated reprinting. *The Rise of Historical Criticism* is interesting to admirers of his work, however, because it shows the development of his style and the wide intellectual range distinguishing the least borné of all the late Victorian writers, with the possible exception of Ruskin. It belongs to Wilde's Oxford days when he was the unsuccessful competitor for the Chancellor's English Essay Prize. Perhaps Magdalen, which has never forgiven herself for nurturing the author of Ravenna, may be felicitated on having escaped the further intolerable honour that she might have suffered by seeing crowned again with paltry academic parsley the most highly gifted of all her children in the last century.

Of the lectures, I have only included those which exist, so far as I know, in manuscript; the reports of others in contemporary newspapers being untrustworthy. They were usually delivered from notes and were repeated at various towns in England and America. Here will be found the origin of Whistler's charges of plagiarism against the author. How far they are justified the reader can decide for himself, Wilde always admitted that, relying on an old and intimate friendship, he asked the artist's assistance on one occasion for a lecture he had failed to prepare in time. This I presume to be the Address delivered to the Art Students of the Royal Academy in 1883, as Whistler certainly reproduced some of it as his own in the 'Ten o'clock' lecture delivered subsequently, in 1885. To what extent an idea may be regarded as a perpetual gift, or whether it is ethically possible to retrieve an idea like an engagement ring, it is not for me to discuss. I would only point out once more that all the works by which Wilde is known throughout Europe were written after the two friends had quarrelled. That Wilde derived a great deal from the older man goes without saying, just as he derived so much in a greater degree from Pater, Ruskin, Arnold and Burne-Jones. Yet the tedious attempt to recognise in every jest of his some original by Whistler induces the criticism that it seems a pity the great painter did not get them off on the public before he was forestalled. Reluctance from an appeal to publicity was never a weakness in either of the men. Some of Wilde's more frequently quoted sayings were made at the Old Bailey (though their provenance is often forgotten) or on his death-bed.

As a matter of fact the genius of the two men was entirely different. Wilde was a humourist and a humanist before everything; and his wittiest jests have neither the relentlessness nor the keenness characterising those of the clever American artist. Again, Whistler could no more have obtained the Berkeley Gold Medal for Greek, nor have written *The Importance of Being Earnest,* and *The Soul of Man,* than Wilde, even if equipped as a painter, could have evinced that superb restraint characterising the portraits of 'Miss Alexander,' 'Carlyle,' and other masterpieces. Wilde, though it is not generally known, was something of a draughtsman in his youth.

Poems in Prose were to have been continued. They are the kind of stories which Wilde would tell at a dinner-table, being invented on the spur of the moment, or inspired by the chance observation of some one who managed to get the traditional word in edgeways; or they were developed from some phrase in a book Wilde might have read during the day. To those who remember hearing them from his lips there must always be a feeling of disappointment on reading them. He overloaded their ornament when he came to transcribe them, and some of his friends did not hesitate to make that criticism to him personally. Though he affected annoyance, I do not think it prevented him from writing the others, which unfortunately exist only in the memories of friends. Miss Aimée Lowther, however, has cleverly noted down some of them in a privately printed volume.

ROBERT ROSS

THE RISE OF HISTORICAL CRITICISM

This Essay was written for the Chancellor's English Essay Prize at Oxford in 1879, the subject being 'Historical Criticism among the Ancients.' The prize was not awarded. To Professor J. W. Mackail thanks are due for revising the proofs.

I

Historical criticism nowhere occurs as an isolated fact in the civilisation or literature of any people. It is part of that complex working towards freedom which may be described as the revolt against authority. It is merely one facet of that speculative spirit of an innovation, which in the sphere of action produces democracy and revolution, and in that of thought is the parent of philosophy and physical science; and its importance as a factor of progress is based not so much on the results it attains, as on the tone of thought which it represents, and the method by which it works.

Being thus the resultant of forces essentially revolutionary, it is not to be found in the ancient world among the material despotisms of Asia or the stationary civilisation of Egypt. The clay cylinders of Assyria and Babylon, the hieroglyphics of the pyramids, form not history but the material for history.

The Chinese annals, ascending as they do to the barbarous forest life of the nation, are marked with a soberness of judgment, a freedom from invention, which is almost unparalleled in the writings of any people; but the protective spirit which is the characteristic of that people proved as fatal to their literature as to their commerce. Free criticism is as unknown as free trade. While as regards the Hindus, their acute, analytical and logical mind is directed rather to grammar, criticism and philosophy than to history or chronology. Indeed, in history their imagination seems to have run wild, legend and fact are so indissolubly mingled together that any attempt to separate them seems vain. If we except the identification of the Greek Sandracottus with the Indian Chandragupta, we have really no clue by which we can test the truth of their writings or examine their method of investigation.

It is among the Hellenic branch of the Indo-Germanic race that history proper is to be found, as well as the spirit of historical criticism; among that wonderful offshoot of the primitive Aryans, whom we call by the name of Greeks and to whom, as has been well said, we owe all that moves in the world except the blind forces of nature.

For, from the day when they left the chill table-lands of Tibet and journeyed, a nomad people, to Ægean shores, the characteristic of their nature has been the search for light, and the spirit of historical criticism is part of that wonderful Aufklärung or illumination of the intellect which seems to have burst on the Greek race like a great flood of light about the sixth century B.C.

L'esprit d'un siècle ne naît pas et ne meurt pas à jour fixe, and the first critic is perhaps as difficult to discover as the first man. It is from democracy that the spirit of criticism borrows its intolerance of dogmatic authority, from physical science the alluring analogies of law and order, from philosophy the conception of an essential unity underlying the complex manifestations of phenomena. It appears first rather as a changed attitude of mind than as a principle of research, and its earliest influences are to be found in the sacred writings.

For men begin to doubt in questions of religion first, and then in matters of more secular interest; and as regards the nature of the spirit of historical criticism itself in its ultimate development, it is not confined merely to the empirical method of ascertaining whether an event happened or not, but is concerned also with the investigation into the causes of events, the general relations which phenomena of life hold to one another, and in its ultimate development passes into the wider question of the philosophy of history.

Now, while the workings of historical criticism in these two spheres of sacred and uninspired history are essentially manifestations of the same spirit, yet their methods are so different, the canons of evidence so entirely separate, and the motives in each case so unconnected, that it will be necessary for a clear estimation of the progress of Greek thought, that we should consider these two questions entirely apart from one another. I shall then in both cases take the succession of writers in their chronological order as representing the rational order—not that the succession of time is always the succession of ideas, or that dialectics moves ever in the straight line in which Hegel conceives its advance. In Greek thought, as elsewhere, there are periods of stagnation and apparent retrogression, yet their intellectual development, not merely in the question of historical criticism, but in their art, their poetry and their philosophy, seems so essentially normal, so free from all disturbing external influences, so peculiarly rational, that in following in the footsteps of time we shall really be progressing in the order sanctioned by reason.

II

At an early period in their intellectual development the Greeks reached that critical point in the history of every civilised nation, when speculative invades the domain of revealed truth, when the spiritual ideas of the people can no longer be satisfied by the lower, material conceptions of their inspired writers, and when men find it impossible to pour the new wine of free thought into the old bottles of a narrow and a trammelling creed.

From their Aryan ancestors they had received the fatal legacy of a mythology stained with immoral and monstrous stories which strove to hide the rational order of nature in a chaos of miracles, and to mar by imputed wickedness the perfection of God's nature—a very shirt of Nessos in which the Heracles of rationalism barely escaped annihilation. Now while undoubtedly the speculations of Thales, and the alluring analogies of law and order afforded by physical science, were most important forces in encouraging the rise of the spirit of scepticism, yet it was on its ethical side that the Greek mythology was chiefly open to attack.

It is difficult to shake the popular belief in miracles, but no man will admit sin and immorality as attributes of the Ideal he worships; so the first symptoms of a new order of thought are shown in the passionate outcries of Xenophanes and Heraclitos against the evil things said by Homer of the sons of God; and in the story told of Pythagoras, how that he saw tortured in Hell the 'two founders of Greek theology,' we can recognise the rise of the Aufklärung as clearly as we see the Reformation foreshadowed in the Inferno of Dante.

Any honest belief, then, in the plain truth of these stories soon succumbed before the destructive effects of the a priori ethical criticism of this school; but the orthodox party, as is its custom, found immediately a convenient shelter under the ægis of the doctrine of metaphors and concealed meanings.

To this allegorical school the tale of the fight around the walls of Troy was a mystery, behind which, as behind a veil, were hidden certain moral and physical truths. The contest between Athena and Ares was that eternal contest between rational thought and the brute force of ignorance; the arrows which rattled in the quiver of the 'Far Darter' were no longer the instruments of vengeance shot from the golden bow of the child of God, but the common rays of the sun, which was itself nothing but a mere inert mass of burning metal.

Modern investigation, with the ruthlessness of Philistine analysis, has ultimately brought Helen of Troy down to a symbol of the dawn. There were Philistines among the Greeks also who saw in the ἄναξ ἀδρῶν a mere metaphor for atmospheric power.

Now while this tendency to look for metaphors and hidden meanings must be ranked as one of the germs of historical criticism, yet it was essentially unscientific. Its inherent weakness is clearly pointed out by Plato, who showed that while this theory will no doubt explain many of the current legends, yet, if it is to be appealed to at all, it must be as a universal principle; a position he is by no means prepared to admit.

Like many other great principles it suffered from its disciples, and furnished its own refutation when the web of Penelope was analysed into a metaphor of the rules of formal logic, the warp representing the premises, and the woof the conclusion.

Rejecting, then, the allegorical interpretation of the sacred writings as an essentially dangerous method, proving either too much or too little, Plato himself returns to the earlier mode of attack, and re-writes history with a didactic purpose, laying down certain ethical canons of historical criticism. God is good; God is just; God is true; God is without the common passions of men. These are the tests to which we are to bring the stories of the Greek religion.

'God predestines no men to ruin, nor sends destruction on innocent cities; He never walks the earth in strange disguise, nor has to mourn for the death of any well-beloved son. Away with the tears for Sarpedon, the lying dream sent to Agamemnon, and the story of the broken covenant!' (Plato, Republic, Book ii. 380; iii. 388, 391.)

Similar ethical canons are applied to the accounts of the heroes of the days of old, and by the same a priori principles Achilles is rescued from the charges of avarice and insolence in a passage which may be recited as the earliest instance of that 'whitewashing of great men,' as it has been called, which is so popular in our own day, when Catiline and Clodius are represented as honest and far-seeing politicians, when eine edle und gute Natur is claimed for Tiberius, and Nero is rescued from his heritage of infamy as an accomplished dilettante whose moral aberrations are more than excused by his exquisite artistic sense and charming tenor voice.

But besides the allegorising principle of interpretation, and the ethical reconstruction of history, there was a third theory, which may be called the semi-historical, and which goes by the name of Euhemeros, though he was by no means the first to propound it.

Appealing to a fictitious monument which he declared that he had discovered in the island of Panchaia, and which purported to be a column erected by Zeus, and detailing the incidents of his reign on earth, this shallow thinker attempted to show that the gods and heroes of ancient Greece were 'mere ordinary mortals, whose achievements had been a good deal exaggerated and misrepresented,' and that the proper canon of historical criticism as regards the treatment of myths was to rationalise the incredible, and to present the plausible residuum as actual truth.

To him and his school, the centaurs, for instance, those mythical sons of the storm, strange links between the lives of men and animals, were merely some youths from the village of Nephele in Thessaly, distinguished for their sporting tastes; the 'living harvest of panoplied knights,' which sprang so mystically from the dragon's teeth, a body of mercenary troops supported by the profits on a successful speculation in ivory; and Actæon, an ordinary master of hounds, who, living before the days of subscription, was eaten out of house and home by the expenses of his kennel.

Now, that under the glamour of myth and legend some substratum of historical fact may lie, is a proposition rendered extremely probable by the modern investigations into the workings of the mythopœic spirit in post-Christian times. Charlemagne and Roland, St. Francis and William Tell, are none the less real personages because their histories are filled with much that is fictitious and incredible, but in all cases what is essentially necessary is some external corroboration, such as is afforded by the mention of Roland and Roncesvalles in the chronicles of England, or (in the sphere of Greek legend) by the excavations of Hissarlik. But to rob a mythical narrative of its kernel of supernatural elements, and to present the dry husk thus obtained as historical fact, is, as has been well said, to mistake entirely the true method of investigation and to identify plausibility with truth.

And as regards the critical point urged by Palaiphatos, Strabo, and Polybius, that pure invention on Homer's part is inconceivable, we may without scruple allow it, for myths, like constitutions, grow gradually, and are not formed in a day. But between a poet's deliberate creation and historical accuracy there is a wide field of the mythopœic faculty.

This Euhemeristic theory was welcomed as an essentially philosophical and critical method by the unscientific Romans, to whom it was introduced by the poet Ennius, that pioneer of cosmopolitan Hellenicism, and it continued to characterise the tone of ancient thought on the question of the treatment of mythology till the rise of Christianity, when it was turned by such writers as Augustine and Minucius Felix into a formidable weapon of attack on Paganism. It was then abandoned by all those who still bent the knee to Athena or to Zeus, and a general return, aided by the philosophic mystics of Alexandria, to the allegorising principle of interpretation took place, as the only means of saving the deities of Olympus from the Titan assaults of the new Galilean God. In what vain defence, the statue of Mary set in the heart of the Pantheon can best tell us.

Religions, however, may be absorbed, but they never are disproved, and the stories of the Greek mythology, spiritualised by the purifying influence of Christianity, reappear in many of the southern parts of Europe in our own day. The old fable that the Greek gods took service with the new religion under assumed names has more truth in it than the many care to discover.

Having now traced the progress of historical criticism in the special treatment of myth and legend, I shall proceed to investigate the form in which the same spirit manifested itself as regards what one may term secular history and secular historians. The field traversed will be found to be in some respects the same, but the mental attitude, the spirit, the motive of investigation are all changed.

There were heroes before the son of Atreus and historians before Herodotus, yet the latter is rightly hailed as the father of history, for in him we discover not merely the empirical connection of cause and effect, but that constant reference to Laws, which is the characteristic of the historian proper.

For all history must be essentially universal; not in the sense of comprising all the synchronous events of the past time, but through the universality of the principles employed. And the great conceptions which unify the work of Herodotus are such as even modern thought has not yet rejected. The immediate government of the world by God, the nemesis and punishment which sin and pride invariably bring with them, the revealing of God's purpose to His people by signs and omens, by miracles and by prophecy; these are to Herodotus the laws which govern the phenomena of history. He is essentially the type of supernatural historian; his eyes are ever strained to discern the Spirit of God moving over the face of the waters of life; he is more concerned with final than with efficient causes.

Yet we can discern in him the rise of that historic sense which is the rational antecedent of the science of historical criticism, the φυσικὸν κριτήριον, to use the words of a Greek writer, as opposed to that which comes either τέχνῃ or διδαχῇ.

He has passed through the valley of faith and has caught a glimpse of the sunlit heights of Reason; but like all those who, while accepting the supernatural, yet attempt to apply the canons of rationalism, he is essentially inconsistent. For the better apprehension of the character of this historic sense in Herodotus it will be necessary to examine at some length the various forms of criticism in which it manifests itself.

Such fabulous stories as that of the Phoenix, of the goat-footed men, of the headless beings with eyes in their breasts, of the men who slept six months in the year (τοῦτο οὐκ ἐνδέχομαι ηὴν ἀρχήν), of the wer-wolf of the Neuri, and the like, are entirely rejected by him as being opposed to the ordinary experience of life, and to those natural laws whose universal influence the early Greek physical philosophers had already made known to the world of thought. Other legends, such as the suckling of Cyrus by a bitch, or the feather-rain of northern Europe, are rationalised and explained into a woman's name and a fall of snow. The supernatural origin of the Scythian nation, from the union of Hercules and the monstrous Echidna, is set aside by him for the more probable account that they were a nomad tribe driven by the Massagetæ from Asia; and he appeals to the local names of their country as proof of the fact that the Kimmerians were the original possessors.

But in the case of Herodotus it will be more instructive to pass on from points like these to those questions of general probability, the true apprehension of which depends rather on a certain quality of mind than on any possibility of formulated rules, questions which form no unimportant part of scientific history; for it must be remembered always that the canons of historical criticism are essentially different from those of judicial evidence, for they cannot, like the latter, be made plain to every ordinary mind, but appeal to a certain historical faculty founded on the experience of life. Besides, the rules for the reception of evidence in courts of law are purely stationary, while the science of historical probability is essentially progressive, and changes with the advancing spirit of each age.

Now, of all the speculative canons of historical criticism, none is more important than that which rests on psychological probability.

Arguing from his knowledge of human nature, Herodotus rejects the presence of Helen within the walls of Troy. Had she been there, he says, Priam and his kinsmen would never have been so mad (φρενοβλαβεῖς) as not to give her up, when they and their children and their city were in such peril (ii. 118); and as regards the authority of Homer, some incidental passages in his poem show that he knew of Helen's sojourn in Egypt during the siege, but selected the other story as being a more suitable motive for an epic. Similarly he does not believe that the Alcmæonidæ family, a family who had always been the haters of tyranny (μισοτύραννοι), and to whom, even more than to Harmodios and Aristogeiton, Athens owed its liberty, would ever have been so treacherous as to hold up a shield after the battle of Marathon as a signal for the Persian host to fall on the city. A shield, he acknowledges, was held up, but it could not possibly have been done by such friends of liberty as the house of Alcmæon; nor will he believe that a great king like Rhampsinitus would have sent his daughter κατίσαι ἐπ' οἰκήματος.

Elsewhere he argues from more general considerations of probability; a Greek courtesan like Rhodopis would hardly have been rich enough to build a pyramid, and, besides, on chronological grounds the story is impossible (ii. 134).

In another passage (ii. 63), after giving an account of the forcible entry of the priests of Ares into the chapel of the god's mother, which seems to have been a sort of religious faction fight where sticks were freely used (μάχη ξύλοισι καρτερή), 'I feel sure,' he says, 'that many of them died from getting their heads broken, notwithstanding the assertions of the Egyptian priests to the contrary.' There is also something charmingly naïve in the account he gives of the celebrated Greek swimmer who dived a distance of eighty stadia to give his countrymen warning of the Persian advance. 'If, however,' he says, 'I may offer an opinion on the subject, I would say that he came in a boat.'

There is, of course, something a little trivial in some of the instances I have quoted; but in a writer like Herodotus, who stands on the borderland between faith and rationalism, one likes to note even the most minute instances of the rise of the critical and sceptical spirit of inquiry.

How really strange, at base, it was with him may, I think, be shown by a reference to those passages where he applies rationalistic tests to matters connected with religion. He nowhere, indeed, grapples with the moral and scientific difficulties of the Greek Bible; and where he rejects as incredible the marvellous achievements of Hercules in Egypt, he does so on the express grounds that he had not yet been received among the gods, and so was still subject to the ordinary conditions of mortal life (ἔτι ἄνθρωπον ἐόντα).

Even within these limits, however, his religious conscience seems to have been troubled at such daring rationalism, and the passage (ii. 45) concludes with a pious hope that God will pardon him for having gone so far, the great rationalistic passage being, of course, that in which he rejects the mythical account of the foundation of Dodona. 'How can a dove speak with a human voice?' he asks, and rationalises the bird into a foreign princess.

Similarly he seems more inclined to believe that the great storm at the beginning of the Persian War ceased from ordinary atmospheric causes, and not in consequence of the incantations of the Magians. He calls Melampos, whom the majority of the Greeks looked on as an inspired prophet, 'a clever man who had acquired for himself the art of prophecy'; and as regards the miracle told of the Æginetan statues of the primeval deities of Damia and Auxesia, that they fell on their knees when the sacrilegious Athenians strove to carry them off, 'any one may believe it,' he says, 'who likes, but as for myself, I place no credence in the tale.'

So much then for the rationalistic spirit of historical criticism, as far as it appears explicitly in the works of this great and philosophic writer; but for an adequate appreciation of his position we must also note how conscious he was of the value of documentary evidence, of the use of inscriptions, of the importance of the poets as throwing light on manners and customs as well as on historical incidents. No writer of any age has more vividly recognised the fact that history is a matter of evidence, and that it is as necessary for the historian to state his authority as it is to produce one's witnesses in a court of law.

While, however, we can discern in Herodotus the rise of an historic sense, we must not blind ourselves to the large amount of instances where he receives supernatural influences as part of the ordinary forces of life.

24

Compared to Thucydides, who succeeded him in the development of history, he appears almost like a mediæval writer matched with a modern rationalist. For, contemporary though they were, between these two authors there is an infinite chasm of thought.

The essential difference of their methods may be best illustrated from those passages where they treat of the same subject. The execution of the Spartan heralds, Nicolaos and Aneristos, during the Peloponnesian War is regarded by Herodotus as one of the most supernatural instances of the workings of nemesis and the wrath of an outraged hero; while the lengthened siege and ultimate fall of Troy was brought about by the avenging hand of God desiring to manifest unto men the mighty penalties which always follow upon mighty sins. But Thucydides either sees not, or desires not to see, in either of these events the finger of Providence, or the punishment of wicked doers. The death of the heralds is merely an Athenian retaliation for similar outrages committed by the opposite side; the long agony of the ten years' siege is due merely to the want of a good commissariat in the Greek army; while the fall of the city is the result of a united military attack consequent on a good supply of provisions.

Now, it is to be observed that in this latter passage, as well as elsewhere, Thucydides is in no sense of the word a sceptic as regards his attitude towards the truth of these ancient legends.

Agamemnon and Atreus, Theseus and Eurystheus, even Minos, about whom Herodotus has some doubts, are to him as real personages as Alcibiades or Gylippus. The points in his historical criticism of the past are, first, his rejection of all extra-natural interference, and, secondly, the attributing to these ancient heroes the motives and modes of thought of his own day. The present was to him the key to the explanation of the past, as it was to the prediction of the future.

Now, as regards his attitude towards the supernatural he is at one with modern science. We too know that, just as the primeval coal-beds reveal to us the traces of rain-drops and other atmospheric phenomena similar to those of our own day, so, in estimating the history of the past, the introduction of no force must be allowed whose workings we cannot observe among the phenomena around us. To lay down canons of ultra-historical credibility for the explanation of events which happen to have preceded us by a few thousand years, is as thoroughly unscientific as it is to intermingle preternatural in geological theories.

Whatever the canons of art may be, no difficulty in history is so great as to warrant the introduction of a spirit of spirit θεὸς ἀπὸ μηχανῆς, in the sense of a violation of the laws of nature.

Upon the other point, however, Thucydides falls into an anachronism. To refuse to allow the workings of chivalrous and self-denying motives among the knights of the Trojan crusade, because he saw none in the faction-loving Athenian of his own day, is to show an entire ignorance of the various characteristics of human nature developing under different circumstances, and to deny to a primitive chieftain like Agamemnon that authority founded on opinion, to which we give the name of divine right, is to fall into an historical error quite as gross as attributing to Atreus the courting of the populace (τεθεραπευκότα τὸν δῆμον) with a view to the Mycenean throne.

The general method of historical criticism pursued by Thucydides having been thus indicated, it remains to proceed more into detail as regards those particular points where he claims for himself a more rational method of estimating evidence than either the public or his predecessors possessed.

'So little pains,' he remarks, 'do the vulgar take in the investigation of truth, satisfied with their preconceived opinions,' that the majority of the Greeks believe in a Pitanate cohort of the Spartan army and in a double vote being the prerogative of the Spartan kings, neither of which opinions has any foundation in fact. But the chief point on which he lays stress as evincing the 'uncritical way with which men receive legends, even the legends of their own country,' is the entire baselessness of the common Athenian tradition in which Harmodios and Aristogeiton were represented as the patriotic liberators of Athens from the Peisistratid tyranny. So far, he points out, from the love of freedom being their motive, both of them were influenced by merely personal considerations, Aristogeiton being jealous of Hipparchos' attention to Harmodios, then a beautiful boy in the flower of Greek loveliness, while the latter's indignation was aroused by an insult offered to his sister by the prince.

Their motives, then, were personal revenge, while the result of their conspiracy served only to rivet more tightly the chains of servitude which bound Athens to the Peisistratid house, for Hipparchos, whom they killed, was only the tyrant's younger brother, and not the tyrant himself.

To prove his theory that Hippias was the elder, he appeals to the evidence afforded by a public inscription in which his name occurs immediately after that of his father, a point which he thinks shows that he was the eldest, and so the heir. This view he further corroborates by another inscription, on the altar of Apollo, which mentions the children of Hippias and not those of his brothers; 'for it was natural for the eldest to be married first'; and besides this, on the score of general probability he points out that, had Hippias been the younger, he would not have so easily obtained the tyranny on the death of Hipparchos.

Now, what is important in Thucydides, as evinced in the treatment of legend generally, is not the results he arrived at, but the method by which he works. The first great rationalistic historian, he may be said to have paved the way for all those who followed after him, though it must always be remembered that, while the total absence in his pages of all the mystical paraphernalia of the supernatural theory of life is an advance in the progress of rationalism, and an era in scientific history, whose importance could never be over-estimated, yet we find along with it a total absence of any mention of those various social and economical forces which form such important factors in the evolution of the world, and to which Herodotus rightly gave great prominence in his immortal work. The history of Thucydides is essentially one-sided and incomplete. The intricate details of sieges and battles, subjects with which the historian proper has really nothing to do except so far as they may throw light on the spirit of the age, we would readily exchange for some notice of the condition of private society in Athens, or the influence and position of women.

There is an advance in the method of historical criticism; there is an advance in the conception and motive of history itself; for in Thucydides we may discern that natural reaction against the intrusion of didactic and theological considerations into the sphere of the pure intellect, the spirit of which may be found in the Euripidean treatment of tragedy and the later schools of art, as well as in the Platonic conception of science.

History, no doubt, has splendid lessons for our instruction, just as all good art comes to us as the herald of the noblest truth. But, to set before either the painter or the historian the inculcation of moral lessons as an aim to be consciously pursued, is to miss entirely the true motive and characteristic both of art and history, which is in the one case the creation of beauty, in the other the discovery of the laws of the evolution of progress: *Il ne faut demander de l'Art que l'Art, du passé que le passé.*

Herodotus wrote to illustrate the wonderful ways of Providence and the nemesis that falls on sin, and his work is a good example of the truth that nothing can dispense with criticism so much as a moral aim. Thucydides has no creed to preach, no doctrine to prove. He analyses the results which follow inevitably from certain antecedents, in order that on a recurrence of the same crisis men may know how to act.

His object was to discover the laws of the past so as to serve as a light to illumine the future. We must not confuse the recognition of the utility of history with any ideas of a didactic aim. Two points more in Thucydides remain for our consideration: his treatment of the rise of Greek civilisation, and of the primitive condition of Hellas, as well as the question how far can he be said really to have recognised the existence of laws regulating the complex phenomena of life.

III

The investigation into the two great problems of the origin of society and the philosophy of history occupies such an important position in the evolution of Greek thought that, to obtain any clear view of the workings of the critical spirit, it will be necessary to trace at some length their rise and scientific development as evinced not merely in the works of historians proper, but also in the philosophical treatises of Plato and Aristotle. The important position which these two great thinkers occupy in the progress of historical criticism can hardly be over-estimated. I do not mean merely as regards their treatment of the Greek Bible, and Plato's endeavours to purge sacred history of its immorality by the application of ethical canons at the time when Aristotle was beginning to undermine the basis of miracles by his scientific conception of law, but with reference to these two wider questions of the rise of civil institutions and the philosophy of history.

And first, as regards the current theories of the primitive condition of society, there was a wide divergence of opinion in Hellenic society, just as there is now. For while the majority of the orthodox public, of whom Hesiod may be taken as the representative, looked back, as a great many of our own day still do, to a fabulous age of innocent happiness, a bell' età dell' auro, where sin and death were unknown and men and women were like Gods, the foremost men of intellect such as Aristotle and Plato, Æschylus and many of the other poets [29] saw in primitive man 'a few small sparks of humanity preserved on the tops of mountains after some deluge,' 'without an idea of cities, governments or legislation,' 'living the lives of wild beasts in sunless caves,' 'their only law being the survival of the fittest.'

And this, too, was the opinion of Thucydides, whose Archæologia as it is contains a most valuable disquisition on the early condition of Hellas, which it will be necessary to examine at some length.

Now, as regards the means employed generally by Thucydides for the elucidation of ancient history, I have already pointed out how that, while acknowledging that 'it is the tendency of every poet to exaggerate, as it is of every chronicler to seek to be attractive at the expense of truth,' he yet assumes in the thoroughly euhemeristic way, that under the veil of myth and legend there does yet exist a rational basis of fact discoverable by the method of rejecting all supernatural interference as well as any extraordinary motives influencing the actors. It is in complete accordance with this spirit that he appeals, for instance, to the Homeric epithet of ἀφνειός, as applied to Corinth, as a proof of the early commercial prosperity of that city; to the fact of the generic name Hellenes not occurring in the Iliad as a corroboration of his theory of the essentially disunited character of the primitive Greek tribes; and he argues from the line 'O'er many islands and all Argos ruled,' as applied to Agamemnon, that his forces must have been partially naval, 'for Agamemnon's was a continental power, and he could not have been master of any but the adjacent islands, and these would not be many but through the possession of a fleet.'

Anticipating in some measure the comparative method of research, he argues from the fact of the more barbarous Greek tribes, such as the Ætolians and Acarnanians, still carrying arms in his own day, that this custom was the case originally over the whole country. 'The fact,' he says, 'that the people in these parts of Hellas are still living in the old way points to a time when the same mode of life was equally common to all.' Similarly, in another passage, he shows how a corroboration of his theory of the respectable character of piracy in ancient days is afforded by 'the honour with which some of the inhabitants of the continent still regard a successful marauder,' as well as by the fact that the question, 'Are you a pirate?' is a common feature of primitive society as shown in the poets; and finally, after observing how the old Greek custom of wearing belts in gymnastic contests still survived among the more uncivilised Asiatic tribes, he observes that there are many other points in which a likeness may be shown between the life of the primitive Hellenes and that of the barbarians to-day.'

As regards the evidence afforded by ancient remains, while adducing as a proof of the insecure character of early Greek society the fact of their cities [31] being always built at some distance from the sea, yet he is careful to warn us, and the caution ought to be borne in mind by all archæologists, that we have no right to conclude from the scanty remains of any city that its legendary greatness in primitive times was a mere exaggeration. 'We are not justified,' he says, 'in rejecting the tradition of the magnitude of the Trojan armament, because Mycenæ and the other towns of that age seem to us small and insignificant. For, if Lacedæmon was to become desolate, any antiquarian judging merely from its ruins would be inclined to regard the tale of the Spartan hegemony as an idle myth; for the city is a mere collection of villages after the old fashion of Hellas, and has none of those splendid public buildings and temples which characterise Athens, and whose remains, in the case of the latter city, would be so marvellous as to lead the superficial observer into an exaggerated estimate of the Athenian power.' Nothing can be more scientific than the archæological canons laid down, whose truth is strikingly illustrated to any one who has compared the waste fields of the Eurotas plain with the lordly monuments of the Athenian acropolis. [32]

On the other hand, Thucydides is quite conscious of the value of the positive evidence afforded by archæological remains. He appeals, for instance, to the character of the armour found in the Delian tombs and the peculiar mode of sepulture, as corroboration of his theory of the predominance of the Carian element among the primitive islanders, and to the concentration of all the temples either in the Acropolis, or in its immediate vicinity, to the name of ἄστυ by which it was still known, and to the extraordinary sanctity of the spring of water there, as proof that the primitive city was originally confined to the citadel, and the district immediately beneath it (ii. 16). And lastly, in the very opening of his history, anticipating one of the most scientific of modern methods, he points out how in early states of civilisation immense fertility of the soil tends to favour the personal aggrandisement of individuals, and so to stop the normal progress of the country through 'the rise of factions, that endless source of ruin'; and also by the allurements it offers to a foreign invader, to necessitate a continual change of population, one immigration following on another. He exemplifies his theory by pointing to the endless political revolutions that characterised Arcadia, Thessaly and Boeotia, the three richest spots in Greece, as well as by the negative instance of the undisturbed state in primitive time of Attica, which was always remarkable for the dryness and poverty of its soil.

Now, while undoubtedly in these passages we may recognise the first anticipation of many of the most modern principles of research, we must remember how essentially limited is the range of the archæologia, and how no theory at all is offered on the wider questions of the general conditions of the rise and progress of humanity, a problem which is first scientifically discussed in the Republic of Plato.

And at the outset it must be premised that, while the study of primitive man is an essentially inductive science, resting rather on the accumulation of evidence than on speculation, among the Greeks it was prosecuted rather on deductive principles. Thucydides did, indeed, avail himself of the opportunities afforded by the unequal development of civilisation in his own day in Greece, and in the places I have pointed out seems to have anticipated the comparative method. But we do not find later writers availing themselves of the wonderfully accurate and picturesque accounts given by Herodotus of the customs of savage tribes. To take one instance, which bears a good deal on modern questions, we find in the works of this great traveller the gradual and progressive steps in the development of the family life clearly manifested in the mere gregarious herding together of the Agathyrsi, their primitive kinsmanship through women in common, and the rise of a feeling of paternity from a state of polyandry. This tribe stood at that time on that borderland between umbilical relationship and the family which has been such a difficult point for modern anthropologists to find.

The ancient authors, however, are unanimous in insisting that the family is the ultimate unit of society, though, as I have said, an inductive study of primitive races, or even the accounts given of them by Herodotus, would have shown them that the νεοττιὰ ἴδια of a personal household, to use Plato's expression, is really a most complex notion appearing always in a late stage of civilisation, along with recognition of private property and the rights of individualism.

Philology also, which in the hands of modern investigators has proved such a splendid instrument of research, was in ancient days studied on principles too unscientific to be of much use. Herodotus points out that the word Eridanos is essentially Greek in character, that consequently the river supposed to run round the world is probably a mere Greek invention. His remarks, however, on language generally, as in the case of Piromis and the ending of the Persian names, show on what unsound basis his knowledge of language rested.

In the Bacchæ of Euripides there is an extremely interesting passage in which the immoral stories of the Greek mythology are accounted for on the principle of that misunderstanding of words and metaphors to which modern science has given the name of a disease of language. In answer to the impious rationalism of Pentheus—a sort of modern Philistine—Teiresias, who may be termed the Max Müller of the Theban cycle, points out that the story of Dionysus being inclosed in Zeus' thigh really arose from the linguistic confusion between μηρός and ὄμηρος.

On the whole, however—for I have quoted these two instances only to show the unscientific character of early philology—we may say that this important instrument in recreating the history of the past was not really used by the ancients as a means of historical criticism. Nor did the ancients employ that other method, used to such advantage in our own day, by which in the symbolism and formulas of an advanced civilisation we can detect the unconscious survival of ancient customs: for, whereas in the sham capture of the bride at a marriage feast, which was common in Wales till a recent time, we can discern the lingering reminiscence of the barbarous habit of exogamy, the ancient writers saw only the deliberate commemoration of an historical event.

Aristotle does not tell us by what method he discovered that the Greeks used to buy their wives in primitive times, but, judging by his general principles, it was probably through some legend or myth on the subject which lasted to his own day, and not, as we would do, by arguing back from the marriage presents given to the bride and her relatives. [37]

The origin of the common proverb 'worth so many beeves,' in which we discern the unconscious survival of a purely pastoral state of society before the use of metals was known, is ascribed by Plutarch to the fact of Theseus having coined money bearing a bull's head. Similarly, the Amathusian festival, in which a young man imitated the labours of a woman in travail, is regarded by him as a rite instituted in Ariadne's honour, and the Carian adoration of asparagus as a simple commemoration of the adventure of the nymph Perigune. In the first of these we discern the beginning of agnation and kinsmanship through the father, which still lingers in the 'couvee' of New Zealand tribes: while the second is a relic of the totem and fetish worship of plants.

Now, in entire opposition to this modern inductive principle of research stands the philosophic Plato, whose account of primitive man is entirely speculative and deductive.

The origin of society he ascribes to necessity, the mother of all inventions, and imagines that individual man began deliberately to herd together on account of the advantages of the principle of division of labour and the rendering of mutual need.

It must, however, be borne in mind that Plato's object in this whole passage in the Republic was, perhaps, not so much to analyse the conditions of early society as to illustrate the importance of the division of labour, the shibboleth of his political economy, by showing what a powerful factor it must have been in the most primitive as well as in the most complex states of society; just as in the Laws he almost rewrites entirely the history of the Peloponnesus in order to prove the necessity of a balance of power. He surely, I mean, must have recognised himself how essentially incomplete his theory was in taking no account of the origin of family life, the position and influence of women, and other social questions, as well as in disregarding those deeper motives of religion, which are such important factors in early civilisation, and whose influence Aristotle seems to have clearly apprehended, when he says that the aim of primitive society was not merely life but the higher life, and that in the origin of society utility is not the sole motive, but that there is something spiritual in it if, at least, 'spiritual' will bring out the meaning of that complex expression $\tau \grave{o} \, \kappa \alpha \lambda \acute{o} \nu$. Otherwise, the whole account in the Republic of primitive man will always remain as a warning against the intrusion of a priori speculations in the domain appropriate to induction.

Now, Aristotle's theory of the origin of society, like his philosophy of ethics, rests ultimately on the principle of final causes, not in the theological meaning of an aim or tendency imposed from without, but in the scientific sense of function corresponding to organ. 'Nature maketh no thing in vain' is the text of Aristotle in this as in other inquiries. Man being the only animal possessed of the power of rational speech is, he asserts, by nature intended to be social, more so than the bee or any other gregarious animal.

He is $\varphi \acute{u} \sigma \epsilon \iota \, \pi o \lambda \iota \tau \iota \kappa \acute{o} \varsigma$, and the national tendency towards higher forms of perfection brings the 'armed savage who used to sell his wife' to the free independence of a free state, and to the ἰσότης τοῦ ἄρχειν καὶ τοῦ ἄρχεσθαι, which was the test of true citizenship. The stages passed through by humanity start with the family first as the ultimate unit.

The conglomeration of families forms a village ruled by that patriarchal sway which is the oldest form of government in the world, as is shown by the fact that all men count it to be the constitution of heaven, and the villages are merged into the state, and here the progression stops.

For Aristotle, like all Greek thinkers, found his ideal within the walls of the πόλις, yet perhaps in his remark that a united Greece would rule the world we may discern some anticipation of that 'federal union of free states into one consolidated empire' which, more than the πόλις, is to our eyes the ultimately perfect polity.

How far Aristotle was justified in regarding the family as the ultimate unit, with the materials afforded to him by Greek literature, I have already noticed. Besides, Aristotle, I may remark, had he reflected on the meaning of that Athenian law which, while prohibiting marriage with a uterine sister, permitted it with a sister-german, or on the common tradition in Athens that before the time of Cecrops children bore their mothers' names, or on some of the Spartan regulations, could hardly have failed to see the universality of kinsmanship through women in early days, and the late appearance of monandry. Yet, while he missed this point, in common, it must be acknowledged, with many modern writers, such as Sir Henry Maine, it is essentially as an explorer of inductive instances that we recognise his improvement on Plato. The treatise περὶ πολιτείων, did it remain to us in its entirety, would have been one of the most valuable landmarks in the progress of historical criticism, and the first scientific treatise on the science of comparative politics.

A few fragments still remain to us, in one of which we find Aristotle appealing to the authority of an ancient inscription on the 'Disk of Iphitus,' one of the most celebrated Greek antiquities, to corroborate his theory of the Lycurgean revival of the Olympian festival; while his enormous research is evinced in the elaborate explanation he gives of the historical origin of proverbs such as οὐδεὶς μέγας κακὸς ἰχθῦς, of religious songs like the ἴωμεν ἐς Ἀθήνας of the Botticean virgins, or the praises of love and war.

And, finally, it is to be observed how much wider than Plato's his theory of the origin of society is. They both rest on a psychological basis, but Aristotle's recognition of the capacity for progress and the tendency towards a higher life shows how much deeper his knowledge of human nature was.

In imitation of these two philosophers, Polybius gives an account of the origin of society in the opening to his philosophy of history. Somewhat in the spirit of Plato, he imagines that after one of the cyclic deluges which sweep off mankind at stated periods and annihilate all pre-existing civilisation, the few surviving members of humanity coalesce for mutual protection, and, as in the case with ordinary animals, the one most remarkable for physical strength is elected king. In a short time, owing to the workings of sympathy and the desire of approbation, the moral qualities begin to make their appearance, and intellectual instead of bodily excellence becomes the qualification for sovereignty.

Other points, as the rise of law and the like, are dwelt on in a somewhat modern spirit, and although Polybius seems not to have employed the inductive method of research in this question, or rather, I should say, of the hierarchical order of the rational progress of ideas in life, he is not far removed from what the laborious investigations of modern travellers have given us.

And, indeed, as regards the working of the speculative faculty in the creation of history, it is in all respects marvellous how that the most truthful accounts of the passage from barbarism to civilisation in ancient literature come from the works of poets. The elaborate researches of Mr. Tylor and Sir John Lubbock have done little more than verify the theories put forward in the Prometheus Bound and the De Natura Rerum; yet neither Æschylus nor Lucretias followed in the modern path, but rather attained to truth by a certain almost mystic power of creative imagination, such as we now seek to banish from science as a dangerous power, though to it science seems to owe many of its most splendid generalities. [43]

Leaving then the question of the origin of society as treated by the ancients, I shall now turn to the other and the more important question of how far they may he said to have attained to what we call the philosophy of history.

Now at the outset we must note that, while the conceptions of law and order have been universally received as the governing principles of the phenomena of nature in the sphere of physical science, yet their intrusion into the domain of history and the life of man has always been met with a strong opposition, on the ground of the incalculable nature of two great forces acting on human action, a certain causeless spontaneity which men call free will, and the extra-natural interference which they attribute as a constant attribute to God.

Now, that there is a science of the apparently variable phenomena of history is a conception which we have perhaps only recently begun to appreciate; yet, like all other great thoughts, it seems to have come to the Greek mind spontaneously, through a certain splendour of imagination, in the morning tide of their civilisation, before inductive research had armed them with the instruments of verification. For I think it is possible to discern in some of the mystic speculations of the early Greek thinkers that desire to discover what is that 'invariable existence of which there are variable states,' and to incorporate it in some one formula of law which may serve to explain the different manifestations of all organic bodies, man included, which is the germ of the philosophy of history; the germ indeed of an idea of which it is not too much to say that on it any kind of historical criticism, worthy of the name, must ultimately rest.

For the very first requisite for any scientific conception of history is the doctrine of uniform sequence: in other words, that certain events having happened, certain other events corresponding to them will happen also; that the past is the key of the future.

Now at the birth of this great conception science, it is true, presided, yet religion it was which at the outset clothed it in its own garb, and familiarised men with it by appealing to their hearts first and then to their intellects;

knowing that at the beginning of things it is through the moral nature, and not through the intellectual, that great truths are spread.

So in Herodotus, who may be taken as a representative of the orthodox tone of thought, the idea of the uniform sequence of cause and effect appears under the theological aspect of Nemesis and Providence, which is really the scientific conception of law, only it is viewed from an ethical standpoint.

Now in Thucydides the philosophy of history rests on the probability, which the uniformity of human nature affords us, that the future will in the course of human things resemble the past, if not reproduce it. He appears to contemplate a recurrence of the phenomena of history as equally certain with a return of the epidemic of the Great Plague.

Notwithstanding what German critics have written on the subject, we must beware of regarding this conception as a mere reproduction of that cyclic theory of events which sees in the world nothing but the regular rotation of Strophe and Antistrophe, in the eternal choir of life and death.

For, in his remarks on the excesses of the Corcyrean Revolution, Thucydides distinctly rests his idea of the recurrence of history on the psychological grounds of the general sameness of mankind.

'The sufferings,' he says, 'which revolution entailed upon the cities were many and terrible, such as have occurred and always will occurs as long as human nature remains the same, though in a severer or milder form, and varying in their symptoms according to the variety of the particular cases.

'In peace and prosperity states and individuals have better sentiments, because they are not confronted with imperious necessities; but war takes away the easy supply of men's wants, and so proves a hard taskmaster, which brings most men's characters to a level with their fortunes.'

IV

It is evident that here Thucydides is ready to admit the variety of manifestations which external causes bring about in their workings on the uniform character of the nature of man. Yet, after all is said, these are perhaps but very general statements: the ordinary effects of peace and war are dwelt on, but there is no real analysis of the immediate causes and general laws of the phenomena of life, nor does Thucydides seem to recognise the truth that if humanity proceeds in circles, the circles are always widening.

Perhaps we may say that with him the philosophy of history is partly in the metaphysical stage, and see, in the progress of this idea from Herodotus to Polybius, the exemplification of the Comtian Law of the three stages of thought, the theological, the metaphysical, and the scientific: for truly out of the vagueness of theological mysticism this conception which we call the Philosophy of History was raised to a scientific principle, according to which the past was explained and the future predicted by reference to general laws.

Now, just as the earliest account of the nature of the progress of humanity is to be found in Plato, so in him we find the first explicit attempt to found a universal philosophy of history upon wide rational grounds. Having created an ideally perfect state, the philosopher proceeds to give an elaborate theory of the complex causes which produce revolutions, of the moral effects of various forms of government and education, of the rise of the criminal classes and their connection with pauperism, and, in a word, to create history by the deductive method and to proceed from a priori psychological principles to discover the governing laws of the apparent chaos of political life.

There have been many attempts since Plato to deduce from a single philosophical principle all the phenomena which experience subsequently verifies for us. Fichte thought he could predict the world-plan from the idea of universal time. Hegel dreamed he had found the key to the mysteries of life in the development of freedom, and Krause in the categories of being. But the one scientific basis on which the true philosophy of history must rest is the complete knowledge of the laws of human nature in all its wants, its aspirations, its powers and its tendencies: and this great truth, which Thucydides may be said in some measure to have apprehended, was given to us first by Plato.

Now, it cannot be accurately said of this philosopher that either his philosophy or his history is entirely and simply a priori. *On est de son siècle même quand on y proteste,* and so we find in him continual references to the

Spartan mode of life, the Pythagorean system, the general characteristics of Greek tyrannies and Greek democracies. For while, in his account of the method of forming an ideal state, he says that the political artist is indeed to fix his gaze on the sun of abstract truth in the heavens of the pure reason, but is sometimes to turn to the realisation of the ideals on earth: yet, after all, the general character of the Platonic method, which is what we are specially concerned with, is essentially deductive and *a priori*. And he himself, in the building up of his Nephelococcygia, certainly starts with a καθαρὸς πίναξ, making a clean sweep of all history and all experience; and it was essentially as an *a priori* theorist that he is criticised by Aristotle, as we shall see later.

To proceed to closer details regarding the actual scheme of the laws of political revolutions as drawn out by Plato, we must first note that the primary cause of the decay of the ideal state is the general principle, common to the vegetable and animal worlds as well as to the world of history, that all created things are fated to decay—a principle which, though expressed in the terms of a mere metaphysical abstraction, is yet perhaps in its essence scientific. For we too must hold that a continuous redistribution of matter and motion is the inevitable result of the nominal persistence of Force, and that perfect equilibrium is as impossible in politics as it certainly is in physics.

The secondary causes which mar the perfection of the Platonic 'city of the sun' are to be found in the intellectual decay of the race consequent on injudicious marriages and in the Philistine elevation of physical achievements over mental culture; while the hierarchical succession of Timocracy and Oligarchy, Democracy and Tyranny, is dwelt on at great length and its causes analysed in a very dramatic and psychological manner, if not in that sanctioned by the actual order of history.

And indeed it is apparent at first sight that the Platonic succession of states represents rather the succession of ideas in the philosophic mind than any historical succession of time.

Aristotle meets the whole simply by an appeal to facts. If the theory of the periodic decay of all created things, he urges, be scientific, it must be universal, and so true of all the other states as well as of the ideal. Besides, a state usually changes into its contrary and not to the form next to it; so the ideal state would not change into Timocracy; while Oligarchy, more often than Tyranny, succeeds Democracy. Plato, besides, says nothing of what a Tyranny would change to. According to the cycle theory it ought to pass into the ideal state again, but as a fact one Tyranny is changed into another as at Sicyon, or into a Democracy as at Syracuse, or into an Aristocracy as at Carthage. The example of Sicily, too, shows that an Oligarchy is often followed by a Tyranny, as at Leontini and Gela. Besides, it is absurd to represent greed as the chief motive of decay, or to talk of avarice as the root of Oligarchy, when in nearly all true oligarchies money-making is forbidden by law. And finally the Platonic theory neglects the different kinds of democracies and of tyrannies.

Now nothing can be more important than this passage in Aristotle's Politics (v. 12.), which may he said to mark an era in the evolution of historical criticism. For there is nothing on which Aristotle insists so strongly as that the generalisations from facts ought to be added to the data of the a priori method—a principle which we know to be true not merely of deductive speculative politics but of physics also: for are not the residual phenomena of chemists a valuable source of improvement in theory?

His own method is essentially historical though by no means empirical. On the contrary, this far-seeing thinker, rightly styled il maestro di color che sanno, may be said to have apprehended clearly that the true method is neither exclusively empirical nor exclusively speculative, but rather a union of both in the process called Analysis or the Interpretation of Facts, which has been defined as the application to facts of such general conceptions as may fix the important characteristics of the phenomena, and present them permanently in their true relations. He too was the first to point out, what even in our own day is incompletely appreciated, that nature, including the development of man, is not full of incoherent episodes like a bad tragedy, that inconsistency and anomaly are as impossible in the moral as they are in the physical world, and that where the superficial observer thinks he sees a revolution the philosophical critic discerns merely the gradual and rational evolution of the inevitable results of certain antecedents.

And while admitting the necessity of a psychological basis for the philosophy of history, he added to it the important truth that man, to be apprehended in his proper position in the universe as well as in his natural powers, must be studied from below in the hierarchical progression of higher function from the lower forms of life. The important maxim, that to obtain a clear conception of anything we must 'study it in its growth from the very beginning,' is formally set down in the opening of the Politics, where, indeed, we shall find the other characteristic features of the modern Evolutionary theory, such as the 'Differentiation of Function' and the 'Survival of the Fittest' explicitly set forth.

What a valuable step this was in the improvement of the method of historical criticism it is needless to point out. By it, one may say, the true thread was given to guide one's steps through the bewildering labyrinth of facts. For history (to use terms with which Aristotle has made us familiar) may be looked at from two essentially different standpoints; either as a work of art whose τέλος or final cause is external to it and imposed on it from without; or as an organism containing the law of its own development in itself, and working out its perfection merely by the fact of being what it is. Now, if we adopt the former, which we may style the theological view, we shall be in continual danger of tripping into the pitfall of some a priori conclusion—that bourne from which, it has been truly said, no traveller ever returns.

The latter is the only scientific theory and was apprehended in its fulness by Aristotle, whose application of the inductive method to history, and whose employment of the evolutionary theory of humanity, show that he was conscious that the philosophy of history is nothing separate from the facts of history but is contained in them, and that the rational law of the complex phenomena of life, like the ideal in the world of thought, is to be reached through the facts, not superimposed on them—κατὰ πολλῶν not παρὰ πολλά.

And finally, in estimating the enormous debt which the science of historical criticism owes to Aristotle, we must not pass over his attitude towards those two great difficulties in the formation of a philosophy of history on which I have touched above. I mean the assertion of extra-natural interference with the normal development of the world and of the incalculable influence exercised by the power of free will.

Now, as regards the former, he may be said to have neglected it entirely. The special acts of providence proceeding from God's immediate government of the world, which Herodotus saw as mighty landmarks in history, would have been to him essentially disturbing elements in that universal reign of law, the extent of whose limitless empire he of all the great thinkers of antiquity was the first explicitly to recognise.

Standing aloof from the popular religion as well as from the deeper conceptions of Herodotus and the Tragic School, he no longer thought of God as of one with fair limbs and treacherous face haunting wood and glade, nor would he see in him a jealous judge continually interfering in the world's history to bring the wicked to punishment and the proud to a fall. God to him was the incarnation of the pure Intellect, a being whose activity was the contemplation of his own perfection, one whom Philosophy might imitate but whom prayers could never move, to the sublime indifference of whose passionless wisdom what were the sons of men, their desires or their sins? While, as regards the other difficulty and the formation of a philosophy of history, the conflict of free will with general laws appears first in Greek thought in the usual theological form in which all great ideas seem to be cradled at their birth.

It was such legends as those of Œdipus and Adrastus, exemplifying the struggles of individual humanity against the overpowering force of circumstances and necessity, which gave to the early Greeks those same lessons which we of modern days draw, in somewhat less artistic fashion, from the study of statistics and the laws of physiology.

In Aristotle, of course, there is no trace of supernatural influence. The Furies, which drive their victim into sin first and then punishment, are no longer 'viper-tressed goddesses with eyes and mouth aflame,' but those evil thoughts which harbour within the impure soul. In this, as in all other points, to arrive at Aristotle is to reach the pure atmosphere of scientific and modern thought.

But while he rejected pure necessitarianism in its crude form as essentially a reductio ad absurdum of life, he was fully conscious of the fact that the will is not a mysterious and ultimate unit of force beyond which we cannot go and whose special characteristic is inconsistency, but a certain creative attitude of the mind which is, from the first, continually influenced by habits, education and circumstance; so absolutely modifiable, in a word, that the good and the bad man alike seem to lose the power of free will; for the one is morally unable to sin, the other physically incapacitated for reformation.

And of the influence of climate and temperature in forming the nature of man (a conception perhaps pressed too far in modern days when the 'race theory' is supposed to be a sufficient explanation of the Hindoo, and the latitude and longitude of a country the best guide to its morals [57]) Aristotle is completely unaware. I do not allude to such smaller points as the oligarchical tendencies of a horse-breeding country and the democratic influence of the proximity of the sea (important though they are for the consideration of Greek history), but rather to those wider views in the seventh book of his Politics, where he attributes the happy union in the Greek character of intellectual attainments with the spirit of progress to the temperate climate they enjoyed, and points out how the extreme cold of the north dulls the mental faculties of its inhabitants and renders them incapable of social organisation or extended empire; while to the enervating heat of eastern countries was due that want of spirit and bravery which then, as now, was the characteristic of the population in that quarter of the globe.

Thucydides has shown the causal connection between political revolutions and the fertility of the soil, but goes a step farther and points out the psychological influences on a people's character exercised by the various extremes of climate—in both cases the first appearance of a most valuable form of historical criticism.

To the development of Dialectic, as to God, intervals of time are of no account. From Plato and Aristotle we pass direct to Polybius.

The progress of thought from the philosopher of the Academe to the

Arcadian historian may be best illustrated by a comparison of the method by which each of the three writers, whom I have selected as the highest expression of the rationalism of his respective age, attained to his ideal state: for the latter conception may be in a measure regarded as representing the most spiritual principle which they could discern in history.

Now, Plato created his on a priori principles; Aristotle formed his by an analysis of existing constitutions; Polybius found his realised for him in the actual world of fact. Aristotle criticised the deductive speculations of Plato by means of inductive negative instances, but Polybius will not take the 'Cloud City' of the Republic into account at all. He compares it to an athlete who has never run on 'Constitution Hill,' to a statue so beautiful that it is entirely removed from the ordinary conditions of humanity, and consequently from the canons of criticism.

The Roman state had attained in his eyes, by means of the mutual counteraction of three opposing forces, [59] that stable equilibrium in politics which was the ideal of all the theoretical writers of antiquity. And in connection with this point it will be convenient to notice here how much truth there is contained in the accusation often brought against the ancients that they knew nothing of the idea of Progress, for the meaning of many of their speculations will be hidden from us if we do not try and comprehend first what their aim was, and secondly why it was so.

Now, like all wide generalities, this statement is at least inaccurate. The prayer of Plato's ideal City—$\dot{\varepsilon}\xi$ $\dot{\alpha}\gamma\alpha\theta\tilde{\omega}\nu$ $\dot{\alpha}\mu\varepsilon\dot{\iota}\nu\sigma\nu\varsigma$, $\kappa\alpha\dot{\iota}$ $\dot{\varepsilon}\xi$ $\dot{\omega}\varphi\varepsilon\lambda\iota\mu\tilde{\omega}\nu$ $\dot{\omega}\varphi\varepsilon\lambda\iota\mu\omega\tau\dot{\varepsilon}\rho\sigma\nu\varsigma$ $\dot{\alpha}\varepsilon\dot{\iota}$ $\tau\sigma\dot{\nu}\varsigma$ $\dot{\varepsilon}\kappa\gamma\dot{\sigma}\nu\sigma\nu\varsigma$ $\gamma\dot{\iota}\gamma\nu\varepsilon\sigma\theta\alpha\iota$, might be written as a text over the door of the last Temple to Humanity raised by the disciples of Fourier and Saint-Simon, but it is certainly true that their ideal principle was order and permanence, not indefinite progress. For, setting aside the artistic prejudices which would have led the Greeks to reject this idea of unlimited improvement, we may note that the modern conception of progress rests partly on the new enthusiasm and worship of humanity, partly on the splendid hopes of material improvements in civilisation which applied science has held out to us, two influences from which ancient Greek thought seems to have been strangely free. For the Greeks marred the perfect humanism of the great men whom they worshipped, by imputing to them divinity and its supernatural powers; while their science was eminently speculative and often almost mystic in its character, aiming at culture and not utility, at higher spirituality and more intense reverence for law, rather than at the increased facilities of locomotion and the cheap production of common things about which our modern scientific school ceases not to boast. And lastly, and perhaps chiefly, we must remember that the 'plague spot of all Greek states,' as one of their own writers has called it, was the terrible insecurity to life and property which resulted from the factions and revolutions which ceased not to trouble Greece at all times, raising a spirit of fanaticism such as religion raised in the middle ages of Europe.

These considerations, then, will enable us to understand first how it was that, radical and unscrupulous reformers as the Greek political theorists were, yet, their end once attained, no modern conservatives raised such outcry against the slightest innovation. Even acknowledged improvements in such things as the games of children or the modes of music were regarded by them with feelings of extreme apprehension as the herald of the drapeau rouge of reform. And secondly, it will show us how it was that Polybius found his ideal in the commonwealth of Rome, and Aristotle, like Mr. Bright, in the middle classes. Polybius, however, is not content merely with pointing out his ideal state, but enters at considerable length into the question of those general laws whose consideration forms the chief essential of the philosophy of history.

He starts by accepting the general principle that all things are fated to decay (which I noticed in the case of Plato), and that 'as iron produces rust and as wood breeds the animals that destroy it, so every state has in it the seeds of its own corruption.' He is not, however, content to rest there, but proceeds to deal with the more immediate causes of revolutions, which he says are twofold in nature, either external or internal. Now, the former, depending as they do on the synchronous conjunction of other events outside the sphere of scientific estimation, are from their very character incalculable; but the latter, though assuming many forms, always result from the over-great preponderance of any single element to the detriment of the others, the rational law lying at the base of all varieties of political changes being that stability can result only from the statical equilibrium produced by the counteraction of opposing parts, since the more simple a constitution is the more it is insecure. Plato had pointed out before how the extreme liberty of a democracy always resulted in despotism, but Polybius analyses the law and shows the scientific principles on which it rests.

The doctrine of the instability of pure constitutions forms an important era in the philosophy of history. Its special applicability to the politics of our own day has been illustrated in the rise of the great Napoleon, when the French state had lost those divisions of caste and prejudice, of landed aristocracy and moneyed interest, institutions in which the vulgar see only barriers to Liberty but which are indeed the only possible defences against the coming of that periodic Sirius of politics, the τύραννος ἐκ προστατικῆς ῥίζης.

There is a principle which Tocqueville never wearies of explaining, and which has been subsumed by Mr. Herbert Spencer under that general law common to all organic bodies which we call the Instability of the Homogeneous. The various manifestations of this law, as shown in the normal, regular revolutions and evolutions of the different forms of government, [63a] are expounded with great clearness by Polybius, who claimed for his theory, in the Thucydidean spirit, that it is a κτῆμα ἐς ἀεί, not a mere ἀγώνισμα ἐς τὸ παραχρῆμα, and that a knowledge of it will enable the impartial observer [63b] to discover at any time what period of its constitutional evolution any particular state has already reached and into what form it will be next differentiated, though possibly the exact time of the changes may be more or less uncertain. [63c]

Now in this necessarily incomplete account of the laws of political revolutions as expounded by Polybius enough perhaps has been said to show what is his true position in the rational development of the 'Idea' which I have called the Philosophy of History, because it is the unifying of history. Seen darkly as it is through the glass of religion in the pages of Herodotus, more metaphysical than scientific with Thucydides, Plato strove to seize it by the eagle-flight of speculation, to reach it with the eager grasp of a soul impatient of those slower and surer inductive methods which Aristotle, in his trenchant criticism of his greater master, showed were more brilliant than any vague theory, if the test of brilliancy is truth.

What then is the position of Polybius? Does any new method remain for him? Polybius was one of those many men who are born too late to be original. To Thucydides belongs the honour of being the first in the history of Greek thought to discern the supreme calm of law and order underlying the fitful storms of life, and Plato and Aristotle each represents a great new principle. To Polybius belongs the office—how noble an office he made it his writings show—of making more explicit the ideas which were implicit in his predecessors, of showing that they were of wider applicability and perhaps of deeper meaning than they had seemed before, of examining with more minuteness the laws which they had discovered, and finally of pointing out more clearly than any one had done the range of science and the means it offered for analysing the present and predicting what was to come. His office thus was to gather up what they had left, to give their principles new life by a wider application.

Polybius ends this great diapason of Greek thought. When the Philosophy of history appears next, as in Plutarch's tract on 'Why God's anger is delayed,' the pendulum of thought had swung back to where it began. His theory was introduced to the Romans under the cultured style of Cicero, and was welcomed by them as the philosophical panegyric of their state. The last notice of it in Latin literature is in the pages of Tacitus, who alludes to the stable polity formed out of these elements as a constitution easier to commend than to produce and in no case lasting. Yet Polybius had seen the future with no uncertain eye, and had prophesied the rise of the Empire from the unbalanced power of the ochlocracy fifty years and more before there was joy in the Julian household over the birth of that boy who, born to power as the champion of the people, died wearing the purple of a king.

No attitude of historical criticism is more important than the means by which the ancients attained to the philosophy of history. The principle of heredity can be exemplified in literature as well as in organic life: Aristotle, Plato and Polybius are the lineal ancestors of Fichte and Hegel, of Vico and Cousin, of Montesquieu and Tocqueville.

As my aim is not to give an account of historians but to point out those great thinkers whose methods have furthered the advance of this spirit of historical criticism, I shall pass over those annalists and chroniclers who intervened between Thucydides and Polybius. Yet perhaps it may serve to throw new light on the real nature of this spirit and its intimate connection with all other forms of advanced thought if I give some estimate of the character and rise of those many influences prejudicial to the scientific study of history which cause such a wide gap between these two historians.

Foremost among these is the growing influence of rhetoric and the Isocratean school, which seems to have regarded history as an arena for the display either of pathos or paradoxes, not a scientific investigation into laws.

The new age is the age of style. The same spirit of exclusive attention to form which made Euripides often, like Swinburne, prefer music to meaning and melody to morality, which gave to the later Greek statues that refined effeminacy, that overstrained gracefulness of attitude, was felt in the sphere of history. The rules laid down for historical composition are those relating to the æsthetic value of digressions, the legality of employing more than one metaphor in the same sentence, and the like; and historians are ranked not by their power of estimating evidence but by the goodness of the Greek they write.

I must note also the important influence on literature exercised by Alexander the Great; for while his travels encouraged the more accurate research of geography, the very splendour of his achievements seems to have brought history again into the sphere of romance. The appearance of all great men in the world is followed invariably by the rise of that mythopœic spirit and that tendency to look for the marvellous, which is so fatal to true historical criticism. An Alexander, a Napoleon, a Francis of Assisi and a Mahomet are thought to be outside the limiting conditions of rational law, just as comets were supposed to be not very long ago. While the founding of that city of Alexandria, in which Western and Eastern thought met with such strange result to both, diverted the critical tendencies of the Greek spirit into questions of grammar, philology and the like, the narrow, artificial atmosphere of that University town (as we may call it) was fatal to the development of that independent and speculative spirit of research which strikes out new methods of inquiry, of which historical criticism is one.

The Alexandrines combined a great love of learning with an ignorance of the true principles of research, an enthusiastic spirit for accumulating materials with a wonderful incapacity to use them. Not among the hot sands of Egypt, or the Sophists of Athens, but from the very heart of Greece rises the man of genius on whose influence in the evolution of the philosophy of history I have a short time ago dwelt. Born in the serene and pure air of the clear uplands of Arcadia, Polybius may be said to reproduce in his work the character of the place which gave him birth. For, of all the historians—I do not say of antiquity but of all time—none is more rationalistic than he, none more free from any belief in the 'visions and omens, the monstrous legends, the grovelling superstitions and unmanly craving for the supernatural' (δεισιδαιμονίας ἀγεννοῦς καὶ τερατείας γυναικώδους [68]) which he himself is compelled to notice as the characteristics of some of the historians who preceded him. Fortunate in the land which bore him, he was no less blessed in the wondrous time of his birth. For, representing in himself the spiritual supremacy of the Greek intellect and allied in bonds of chivalrous friendship to the world-conqueror of his day, he seems led as it were by the hand of Fate 'to comprehend,' as has been said, 'more clearly than the Romans themselves the historical position of Rome,' and to discern with greater insight than all other men could those two great resultants of ancient civilisation, the material empire of the city of the seven hills, and the intellectual sovereignty of Hellas.

Before his own day, he says, [69a] the events of the world were unconnected and separate and the histories confined to particular countries. Now, for the first time the universal empire of the Romans rendered a universal history possible. [69b] This, then, is the august motive of his work: to trace the gradual rise of this Italian city from the day when the first legion crossed the narrow strait of Messina and landed on the fertile fields of Sicily to the time when Corinth in the East and Carthage in the West fell before the resistless wave of empire and the eagles of Rome passed on the wings of universal victory from Calpe and the Pillars of Hercules to Syria and the Nile. At the same time he recognised that the scheme of Rome's empire was worked out under the ægis of God's will. [69c] For, as one of the Middle Age scribes most truly says, the τύχη of Polybius is that power which we Christians call God; the second aim, as one may call it, of his history is to point out the rational and human and natural causes which brought this result, distinguishing, as we should say, between God's mediate and immediate government of the world.

With any direct intervention of God in the normal development of Man, he will have nothing to do: still less with any idea of chance as a factor in the phenomena of life. Chance and miracles, he says, are mere expressions for our ignorance of rational causes. The spirit of rationalism which we recognised in Herodotus as a vague uncertain attitude and which appears in Thucydides as a consistent attitude of mind never argued about or even explained, is by Polybius analysed and formulated as the great instrument of historical research.

Herodotus, while believing on principle in the supernatural, yet was sceptical at times. Thucydides simply ignored the supernatural. He did not discuss it, but he annihilated it by explaining history without it. Polybius enters at length into the whole question and explains its origin and the method of treating it. Herodotus would have believed in Scipio's dream. Thucydides would have ignored it entirely. Polybius explains it. He is the culmination of the rational progression of Dialectic. 'Nothing,' he says, 'shows a foolish mind more than the attempt to account for any phenomena on the principle of chance or supernatural intervention. History is a search for rational causes, and there is nothing in the world—even those phenomena which seem to us the most remote from law and improbable—which is not the logical and inevitable result of certain rational antecedents.'

Some things, of course, are to be rejected a priori without entering into the subject: 'As regards such miracles,' he says, [71] 'as that on a certain statue of Artemis rain or snow never falls though the statue stands in the open air, or that those who enter God's shrine in Arcadia lose their natural shadows, I cannot really be expected to argue upon the subject. For these things are not only utterly improbable but absolutely impossible.'

'For us to argue reasonably on an acknowledged absurdity is as vain a task as trying to catch water in a sieve; it is really to admit the possibility of the supernatural, which is the very point at issue.'

What Polybius felt was that to admit the possibility of a miracle is to annihilate the possibility of history: for just as scientific and chemical experiments would be either impossible or useless if exposed to the chance of continued interference on the part of some foreign body, so the laws and principles which govern history, the causes of phenomena, the evolution of progress, the whole science, in a word, of man's dealings with his own race and with nature, will remain a sealed book to him who admits the possibility of extra-natural interference.

The stories of miracles, then, are to be rejected on a priori rational grounds, but in the case of events which we know to have happened the scientific historian will not rest till he has discovered their natural causes which, for instance, in the case of the wonderful rise of the Roman Empire— the most marvellous thing, Polybius says, which God ever brought about [72a]—are to be found in the excellence of their constitution ($\tau\tilde{\eta}$ $\imath\delta\iota\acute{o}\tau\eta\tau\iota$ $\tau\tilde{\eta}\varsigma$ $\pi o\lambda\iota\tau\epsilon\acute{\iota}\alpha\varsigma$), the wisdom of their advisers, their splendid military arrangements, and their superstition ($\tau\tilde{\eta}$ $\delta\epsilon\iota\sigma\iota\delta\alpha\iota\mu o\nu\acute{\iota}\alpha$). For while Polybius regarded the revealed religion as, of course, objective reality of truth, [72b] he laid great stress on its moral subjective influence, going, in one passage on the subject, even so far as almost to excuse the introduction of the supernatural in very small quantities into history on account of the extremely good effect it would have on pious people.

But perhaps there is no passage in the whole of ancient and modern history which breathes such a manly and splendid spirit of rationalism as one preserved to us in the Vatican—strange resting-place for it!—in which he treats of the terrible decay of population which had fallen on his native land in his own day, and which by the general orthodox public was regarded as a special judgment of God sending childlessness on women as a punishment for the sins of the people. For it was a disaster quite without parallel in the history of the land, and entirely unforeseen by any of its political-economy writers who, on the contrary, were always anticipating that danger would arise from an excess of population overrunning its means of subsistence, and becoming unmanageable through its size. Polybius, however, will have nothing to do with either priest or worker of miracles in this matter. He will not even seek that 'sacred Heart of Greece,' Delphi, Apollo's shrine, whose inspiration even Thucydides admitted and before whose wisdom Socrates bowed. How foolish, he says, were the man who on this matter would pray to God. We must search for the rational causes, and the causes are seen to be clear, and the method of prevention also. He then proceeds to notice how all this arose from the general reluctance to marriage and to bearing the expense of educating a large family which resulted from the carelessness and avarice of the men of his day, and he explains on entirely rational principles the whole of this apparently supernatural judgment.

Now, it is to be borne in mind that while his rejection of miracles as violation of inviolable laws is entirely a priori—for discussion of such a matter is, of course, impossible for a rational thinker—yet his rejection of supernatural intervention rests entirely on the scientific grounds of the necessity of looking for natural causes. And he is quite logical in maintaining his position on these principles. For, where it is either difficult or impossible to assign any rational cause for phenomena, or to discover their laws, he acquiesces reluctantly in the alternative of admitting some extra-natural interference which his essentially scientific method of treating the matter has logically forced on him, approving, for instance, of prayers for rain, on the express ground that the laws of meteorology had not yet been ascertained. He would, of course, have been the first to welcome our modern discoveries in the matter. The passage in question is in every way one of the most interesting in his whole work, not, of course, as signifying any inclination on his part to acquiesce in the supernatural, but because it shows how essentially logical and rational his method of argument was, and how candid and fair his mind.

Having now examined Polybius's attitude towards the supernatural and the general ideas which guided his research, I will proceed to examine the method he pursued in his scientific investigation of the complex phenomena of life. For, as I have said before in the course of this essay, what is important in all great writers is not so much the results they arrive at as the methods they pursue. The increased knowledge of facts may alter any conclusion in history as in physical science, and the canons of speculative historical credibility must be acknowledged to appeal rather to that subjective attitude of mind which we call the historic sense than to any formulated objective rules. But a scientific method is a gain for all time, and the true if not the only progress of historical criticism consists in the improvement of the instruments of research.

Now first, as regards his conception of history, I have already pointed out that it was to him essentially a search for causes, a problem to be solved, not a picture to be painted, a scientific investigation into laws and tendencies, not a mere romantic account of startling incident and wondrous adventure. Thucydides, in the opening of his great work, had sounded the first note of the scientific conception of history. 'The absence of romance in my pages,' he says, 'will, I fear, detract somewhat from its value, but I have written my work not to be the exploit of a passing hour but as the possession of all time.' [76] Polybius follows with words almost entirely similar. If, he says, we banish from history the consideration of causes, methods and motives (τὸ διὰ τί, καὶ πως, καὶ τίνος χάριν), and refuse to consider how far the result of anything is its rational consequent, what is left is a mere ἀγώνισμα, not a μάθημα, an oratorical essay which may give pleasure for the moment, but which is entirely without any scientific value for the explanation of the future. Elsewhere he says that 'history robbed of the exposition of its causes and laws is a profitless thing, though it may allure a fool.' And all through his history the same point is put forward and exemplified in every fashion.

So far for the conception of history. Now for the groundwork. As regards the character of the phenomena to be selected by the scientific investigator, Aristotle had laid down the general formula that nature should be studied in her normal manifestations. Polybius, true to his character of applying explicitly the principles implicit in the work of others, follows out the doctrine of Aristotle, and lays particular stress on the rational and undisturbed character of the development of the Roman constitution as affording special facilities for the discovery of the laws of its progress. Political revolutions result from causes either external or internal. The former are mere disturbing forces which lie outside the sphere of scientific calculation.

It is the latter which are important for the establishing of principles and the elucidation of the sequences of rational evolution.

He thus may be said to have anticipated one of the most important truths of the modern methods of investigation: I mean that principle which lays down that just as the study of physiology should precede the study of pathology, just as the laws of disease are best discovered by the phenomena presented in health, so the method of arriving at all great social and political truths is by the investigation of those cases where development has been normal, rational and undisturbed.

The critical canon that the more a people has been interfered with, the more difficult it becomes to generalise the laws of its progress and to analyse the separate forces of its civilisation, is one the validity of which is now generally recognised by those who pretend to a scientific treatment of all history: and while we have seen that Aristotle anticipated it in a general formula, to Polybius belongs the honour of being the first to apply it explicitly in the sphere of history.

I have shown how to this great scientific historian the motive of his work was essentially the search for causes; and true to his analytical spirit he is careful to examine what a cause really is and in what part of the antecedents of any consequent it is to be looked for. To give an illustration: As regards the origin of the war with Perseus, some assigned as causes the expulsion of Abrupolis by Perseus, the expedition of the latter to Delphi, the plot against Eumenes and the seizure of the ambassadors in Bœotia; of these incidents the two former, Polybius points out, were merely the pretexts, the two latter merely the occasions of the war. The war was really a legacy left to Perseus by his father, who was determined to fight it out with Rome. [78]

Here as elsewhere he is not originating any new idea. Thucydides had pointed out the difference between the real and the alleged cause, and the Aristotelian dictum about revolutions, οὐ περὶ μικρῶν ἀλλ' ἐκ μικρῶν, draws the distinction between cause and occasion with the brilliancy of an epigram. But the explicit and rational investigation of the difference between αἰτία, ἀρχὴ, and πρόφασις was reserved for Polybius. No canon

55

of historical criticism can be said to be of more real value than that involved in this distinction, and the overlooking of it has filled our histories with the contemptible accounts of the intrigues of courtiers and of kings and the petty plottings of backstairs influence—particulars interesting, no doubt, to those who would ascribe the Reformation to Anne Boleyn's pretty face, the Persian war to the influence of a doctor or a curtain-lecture from Atossa, or the French Revolution to Madame de Maintenon, but without any value for those who aim at any scientific treatment of history.

But the question of method, to which I am compelled always to return, is not yet exhausted. There is another aspect in which it may be regarded, and I shall now proceed to treat of it.

One of the greatest difficulties with which the modern historian has to contend is the enormous complexity of the facts which come under his notice: D'Alembert's suggestion that at the end of every century a selection of facts should be made and the rest burned (if it was really intended seriously) could not, of course, be entertained for a moment. A problem loses all its value when it becomes simplified, and the world would be all the poorer if the Sibyl of History burned her volumes. Besides, as Gibbon pointed out, 'a Montesquieu will detect in the most insignificant fact relations which the vulgar overlook.'

Nor can the scientific investigator of history isolate the particular elements, which he desires to examine, from disturbing and extraneous causes, as the experimental chemist can do (though sometimes, as in the case of lunatic asylums and prisons, he is enabled to observe phenomena in a certain degree of isolation). So he is compelled either to use the deductive mode of arguing from general laws or to employ the method of abstraction, which gives a fictitious isolation to phenomena never so isolated in actual existence. And this is exactly what Polybius has done as well as Thucydides. For, as has been well remarked, there is in the works of these two writers a certain plastic unity of type and motive; whatever they write is penetrated through and through with a specific quality, a singleness and concentration of purpose, which we may contrast with the more comprehensive width as manifested not merely in the modern mind, but also in Herodotus. Thucydides, regarding society as influenced entirely by political motives, took no account of forces of a different nature, and consequently his results, like those of most modern political economists, have to be modified largely [81] before they come to correspond with what we know was the actual state of fact. Similarly, Polybius will deal only with those forces which tended to bring the civilised world under the dominion of Rome (ix. 1), and in the Thucydidean spirit points out the want of picturesqueness and romance in his pages which is the result of the abstract method ($\tau\grave{o}$ $\mu o\nu o\varepsilon\iota\delta\grave{\varepsilon}\varsigma$ $\tau\tilde{\eta}\varsigma$ $\sigma\upsilon\nu\tau\acute{\alpha}\xi\varepsilon\omega\varsigma$) being careful also to tell us that his rejection of all other forces is essentially deliberate and the result of a preconceived theory and by no means due to carelessness of any kind.

Now, of the general value of the abstract method and the legality of its employment in the sphere of history, this is perhaps not the suitable occasion for any discussion. It is, however, in all ways worthy of note that Polybius is not merely conscious of, but dwells with particular weight on, the fact which is usually urged as the strongest objection to the employment of the abstract method—I mean the conception of a society as a sort of human organism whose parts are indissolubly connected with one another and all affected when one member is in any way agitated. This conception of the organic nature of society appears first in Plato and Aristotle, who apply it to cities. Polybius, as his wont is, expands it to be a general characteristic of all history. It is an idea of the very highest importance, especially to a man like Polybius whose thoughts are continually turned towards the essential unity of history and the impossibility of isolation.

Farther, as regards the particular method of investigating that group of phenomena obtained for him by the abstract method, he will adopt, he tells us, neither the purely deductive nor the purely inductive mode but the union of both. In other words, he formally adopts that method of analysis upon the importance of which I have dwelt before.

And lastly, while, without doubt, enormous simplicity in the elements under consideration is the result of the employment of the abstract method, even within the limit thus obtained a certain selection must be made, and a selection involves a theory. For the facts of life cannot be tabulated with as great an ease as the colours of birds and insects can be tabulated. Now, Polybius points out that those phenomena particularly are to be dwelt on which may serve as a παράδειγμα or sample, and show the character of the tendencies of the age as clearly as 'a single drop from a full cask will be enough to disclose the nature of the whole contents.' This recognition of the importance of single facts, not in themselves but because of the spirit they represent, is extremely scientific; for we know that from the single bone, or tooth even, the anatomist can recreate entirely the skeleton of the primeval horse, and the botanist tell the character of the flora and fauna of a district from a single specimen.

Regarding truth as 'the most divine thing in Nature,' the very 'eye and light of history without which it moves a blind thing,' Polybius spared no pains in the acquisition of historical materials or in the study of the sciences of politics and war, which he considered were so essential to the training of the scientific historian, and the labour he took is mirrored in the many ways in which he criticises other authorities.

There is something, as a rule, slightly contemptible about ancient criticism. The modern idea of the critic as the interpreter, the expounder of the beauty and excellence of the work he selects, seems quite unknown. Nothing can be more captious or unfair, for instance, than the method by which Aristotle criticised the ideal state of Plato in his ethical works, and the passages quoted by Polybius from Timæus show that the latter historian fully deserved the punning name given to him. But in Polybius there is, I think, little of that bitterness and pettiness of spirit which characterises most other writers, and an incidental story he tells of his relations with one of the historians whom he criticised shows that he was a man of great courtesy and refinement of taste—as, indeed, befitted one who had lived always in the society of those who were of great and noble birth.

Now, as regards the character of the canons by which he criticises the works of other authors, in the majority of cases he employs simply his own geographical and military knowledge, showing, for instance, the impossibility in the accounts given of Nabis's march from Sparta simply by his acquaintance with the spots in question; or the inconsistency of those of the battle of Issus;

or of the accounts given by Ephorus of the battles of Leuctra and Mantinea. In the latter case he says, if any one will take the trouble to measure out the ground of the site of the battle and then test the manœuvres given, he will find how inaccurate the accounts are.

In other cases he appeals to public documents, the importance of which he was always foremost in recognising; showing, for instance, by a document in the public archives of Rhodes how inaccurate were the accounts given of the battle of Lade by Zeno and Antisthenes. Or he appeals to psychological probability, rejecting, for instance, the scandalous stories told of Philip of Macedon, simply from the king's general greatness of character, and arguing that a boy so well educated and so respectably connected as Demochares (xii. 14) could never have been guilty of that of which evil rumour accused him.

But the chief object of his literary censure is Timæus, who had been unsparing of his strictures on others. The general point which he makes against him, impugning his accuracy as a historian, is that he derived his knowledge of history not from the dangerous perils of a life of action but in the secure indolence of a narrow scholastic life. There is, indeed, no point on which he is so vehement as this. 'A history,' he says, 'written in a library gives as lifeless and as inaccurate a picture of history as a painting which is copied not from a living animal but from a stuffed one.'

There is more difference, he says in another place, between the history of an eye-witness and that of one whose knowledge comes from books, than there is between the scenes of real life and the fictitious landscapes of theatrical scenery. Besides this, he enters into somewhat elaborate detailed criticism of passages where he thought Timæus was following a wrong method and perverting truth, passages which it will be worth while to examine in detail.

Timæus, from the fact of there being a Roman custom to shoot a war-horse on a stated day, argued back to the Trojan origin of that people. Polybius, on the other hand, points out that the inference is quite unwarrantable, because horse-sacrifices are ordinary institutions common to all barbarous tribes. Timæus here, as was common with Greek writers, is arguing back from some custom of the present to an historical event in the past. Polybius

59

really is employing the comparative method, showing how the custom was an ordinary step in the civilisation of every early people.

In another place, [86] he shows how illogical is the scepticism of Timæus as regards the existence of the Bull of Phalaris simply by appealing to the statue of the Bull, which was still to be seen in Carthage; pointing out how impossible it was, on any other theory except that it belonged to Phalaris, to account for the presence in Carthage of a bull of this peculiar character with a door between his shoulders. But one of the great points which he uses against this Sicilian historian is in reference to the question of the origin of the Locrian colony. In accordance with the received tradition on the subject, Aristotle had represented the Locrian colony as founded by some Parthenidæ or slaves' children, as they were called, a statement which seems to have roused the indignation of Timæus, who went to a good deal of trouble to confute this theory. He does so on the following grounds:—

First of all, he points out that in the ancient days the Greeks had no slaves at all, so the mention of them in the matter is an anachronism; and next he declares that he was shown in the Greek city of Locris certain ancient inscriptions in which their relation to the Italian city was expressed in terms of the position between parent and child, which showed also that mutual rights of citizenship were accorded to each city. Besides this, he appeals to various questions of improbability as regards their international relationship, on which Polybius takes diametrically opposite grounds which hardly call for discussion. And in favour of his own view he urges two points more: first, that the Lacedæmonians being allowed furlough for the purpose of seeing their wives at home, it was unlikely that the Locrians should not have had the same privilege; and next, that the Italian Locrians knew nothing of the Aristotelian version and had, on the contrary, very severe laws against adulterers, runaway slaves and the like. Now, most of these questions rest on mere probability, which is always such a subjective canon that an appeal to it is rarely conclusive. I would note, however, as regards the inscriptions which, if genuine, would of course have settled the matter, that Polybius looks on them as a mere invention on the part of Timæus, who, he remarks, gives no details about them, though, as a rule, he is over-anxious to give chapter and verse for everything. A somewhat more interesting point is that where he attacks Timæus for the introduction of fictitious speeches into his narrative; for on this point Polybius seems to be far in advance of the opinions held by literary men on the subject not merely in his own day, but for centuries after.

Herodotus had introduced speeches avowedly dramatic and fictitious. Thucydides states clearly that, where he was unable to find out what people really said, he put down what they ought to have said. Sallust alludes, it is true, to the fact of the speech he puts into the mouth of the tribune Memmius being essentially genuine, but the speeches given in the senate on the occasion of the Catilinarian conspiracy are very different from the same orations as they appear in Cicero. Livy makes his ancient Romans wrangle and chop logic with all the subtlety of a Hortensius or a Scævola. And even in later days, when shorthand reporters attended the debates of the senate and a Daily News was published in Rome, we find that one of the most celebrated speeches in Tacitus (that in which the Emperor Claudius gives the Gauls their freedom) is shown, by an inscription discovered recently at Lugdunum, to be entirely fabulous.

Upon the other hand, it must be borne in mind that these speeches were not intended to deceive; they were regarded merely as a certain dramatic element which it was allowable to introduce into history for the purpose of giving more life and reality to the narration, and were to be criticised, not as we should, by arguing how in an age before shorthand was known such a report was possible or how, in the failure of written documents, tradition could bring down such an accurate verbal account, but by the higher test of their psychological probability as regards the persons in whose mouths they are placed. An ancient historian in answer to modern criticism would say, probably, that these fictitious speeches were in reality more truthful than the actual ones, just as Aristotle claimed for poetry a higher degree of truth in comparison to history. The whole point is interesting as showing how far in advance of his age Polybius may be said to have been.

The last scientific historian, it is possible to gather from his writings what he considered were the characteristics of the ideal writer of history; and no small light will be thrown on the progress of historical criticism if we strive

61

to collect and analyse what in Polybius are more or less scattered expressions. The ideal historian must be contemporary with the events he describes, or removed from them by one generation only. Where it is possible, he is to be an eye-witness of what he writes of; where that is out of his power he is to test all traditions and stories carefully and not to be ready to accept what is plausible in place of what is true. He is to be no bookworm living aloof from the experiences of the world in the artificial isolation of a university town, but a politician, a soldier, and a traveller, a man not merely of thought but of action, one who can do great things as well as write of them, who in the sphere of history could be what Byron and Æschylus were in the sphere of poetry, at once le chantre et le héros.

He is to keep before his eyes the fact that chance is merely a synonym for our ignorance; that the reign of law pervades the domain of history as much as it does that of political science. He is to accustom himself to look on all occasions for rational and natural causes. And while he is to recognise the practical utility of the supernatural, in an educational point of view, he is not himself to indulge in such intellectual beating of the air as to admit the possibility of the violation of inviolable laws, or to argue in a sphere wherein argument is a priori annihilated. He is to be free from all bias towards friend and country; he is to be courteous and gentle in criticism; he is not to regard history as a mere opportunity for splendid and tragic writing; nor is he to falsify truth for the sake of a paradox or an epigram.

While acknowledging the importance of particular facts as samples of higher truths, he is to take a broad and general view of humanity. He is to deal with the whole race and with the world, not with particular tribes or separate countries. He is to bear in mind that the world is really an organism wherein no one part can be moved without the others being affected also. He is to distinguish between cause and occasion, between the influence of general laws and particular fancies, and he is to remember that the greatest lessons of the world are contained in history and that it is the historian's duty to manifest them so as to save nations from following those unwise policies which always lead to dishonour and ruin, and to teach individuals to apprehend by the intellectual culture of history those truths which else they would have to learn in the bitter school of experience.

Now, as regards his theory of the necessity of the historian's being contemporary with the events he describes, so far as the historian is a mere narrator the remark is undoubtedly true. But to appreciate the harmony and rational position of the facts of a great epoch, to discover its laws, the causes which produced it and the effects which it generates, the scene must be viewed from a certain height and distance to be completely apprehended. A thoroughly contemporary historian such as Lord Clarendon or Thucydides is in reality part of the history he criticises; and, in the case of such contemporary historians as Fabius and Philistus, Polybius in compelled to acknowledge that they are misled by patriotic and other considerations. Against Polybius himself no such accusation can be made. He indeed of all men is able, as from some lofty tower, to discern the whole tendency of the ancient world, the triumph of Roman institutions and of Greek thought which is the last message of the old world and, in a more spiritual sense, has become the Gospel of the new.

One thing indeed he did not see, or if he saw it, he thought but little of it—how from the East there was spreading over the world, as a wave spreads, a spiritual inroad of new religions from the time when the Pessinuntine mother of the gods, a shapeless mass of stone, was brought to the eternal city by her holiest citizen, to the day when the ship Castor and Pollux stood in at Puteoli, and St. Paul turned his face towards martyrdom and victory at Rome. Polybius was able to predict, from his knowledge of the causes of revolutions and the tendencies of the various forms of governments, the uprising of that democratic tone of thought which, as soon as a seed is sown in the murder of the Gracchi and the exile of Marius, culminated as all democratic movements do culminate, in the supreme authority of one man, the lordship of the world under the world's rightful lord, Caius Julius Cæsar. This, indeed, he saw in no uncertain way. But the turning of all men's hearts to the East, the first glimmering of that splendid dawn which broke over the hills of Galilee and flooded the earth like wine, was hidden from his eyes.

There are many points in the description of the ideal historian which one may compare to the picture which Plato has given us of the ideal philosopher. They are both 'spectators of all time and all existence.' Nothing is contemptible in their eyes, for all things have a meaning, and they both walk in august reasonableness before all men, conscious of the workings of God yet free from all terror of mendicant priest or vagrant miracle-worker. But the parallel ends here. For the one stands aloof from the world-storm of sleet and hail, his eyes fixed on distant and sunlit heights, loving knowledge for the sake of knowledge and wisdom for the joy of wisdom, while the other is an eager actor in the world ever seeking to apply his knowledge to useful things. Both equally desire truth, but the one because of its utility, the other for its beauty. The historian regards it as the rational principle of all true history, and no more. To the other it comes as an all-pervading and mystic enthusiasm, 'like the desire of strong wine, the craving of ambition, the passionate love of what is beautiful.'

Still, though we miss in the historian those higher and more spiritual qualities which the philosopher of the Academe alone of all men possessed, we must not blind ourselves to the merits of that great rationalist who seems to have anticipated the very latest words of modern science. Nor yet is he to be regarded merely in the narrow light in which he is estimated by most modern critics, as the explicit champion of rationalism and nothing more. For he is connected with another idea, the course of which is as the course of that great river of his native Arcadia which, springing from some arid and sun-bleached rock, gathers strength and beauty as it flows till it reaches the asphodel meadows of Olympia and the light and laughter of Ionian waters.

For in him we can discern the first notes of that great cult of the seven-hilled city which made Virgil write his epic and Livy his history, which found in Dante its highest exponent, which dreamed of an Empire where the Emperor would care for the bodies and the Pope for the souls of men, and so has passed into the conception of God's spiritual empire and the universal brotherhood of man and widened into the huge ocean of universal thought as the Peneus loses itself in the sea.

Polybius is the last scientific historian of Greece. The writer who seems fittingly to complete the progress of thought is a writer of biographies only. I will not here touch on Plutarch's employment of the inductive method as shown in his constant use of inscription and statue, of public document and building and the like, because it involves no new method. It is his attitude towards miracles of which I desire to treat.

Plutarch is philosophic enough to see that in the sense of a violation of the laws of nature a miracle is impossible. It is absurd, he says, to imagine that the statue of a saint can speak, and that an inanimate object not possessing the vocal organs should be able to utter an articulate sound. Upon the other hand, he protests against science imagining that, by explaining the natural causes of things, it has explained away their transcendental meaning. 'When the tears on the cheek of some holy statue have been analysed into the moisture which certain temperatures produce on wood and marble, it yet by no means follows that they were not a sign of grief and mourning set there by God Himself.' When Lampon saw in the prodigy of the one-horned ram the omen of the supreme rule of Pericles, and when Anaxagoras showed that the abnormal development was the rational resultant of the peculiar formation of the skull, the dreamer and the man of science were both right; it was the business of the latter to consider how the prodigy came about, of the former to show why it was so formed and what it so portended. The progression of thought is exemplified in all particulars. Herodotus had a glimmering sense of the impossibility of a violation of nature. Thucydides ignored the supernatural. Polybius rationalised it. Plutarch raises it to its mystical heights again, though he bases it on law. In a word, Plutarch felt that while science brings the supernatural down to the natural, yet ultimately all that is natural is really supernatural. To him, as to many of our own day, religion was that transcendental attitude of the mind which, contemplating a world resting on inviolable law, is yet comforted and seeks to worship God not in the violation but in the fulfilment of nature.

It may seem paradoxical to quote in connection with the priest of Chæronea such a pure rationalist as Mr. Herbert Spencer; yet when we read as the last message of modern science that 'when the equation of life has been reduced to its lowest terms the symbols are symbols still,' mere signs, that is, of that unknown reality which underlies all matter and all spirit, we may feel how over the wide strait of centuries thought calls to thought and how Plutarch has a higher position than is usually claimed for him in the progress of the Greek intellect.

And, indeed, it seems that not merely the importance of Plutarch himself but also that of the land of his birth in the evolution of Greek civilisation has been passed over by modern critics. To us, indeed, the bare rock to which the Parthenon serves as a crown, and which lies between Colonus and Attica's violet hills, will always be the holiest spot in the land of Greece: and Delphi will come next, and then the meadows of Eurotas where that noble people lived who represented in Hellenic thought the reaction of the law of duty against the law of beauty, the opposition of conduct to culture. Yet, as one stands on the σχιστὴ ὁδός of Cithæron and looks out on the great double plain of Boeotia, the enormous importance of the division of Hellas comes to one's mind with great force. To the north are Orchomenus and the Minyan treasure-house, seat of those merchant princes of Phoenicia who brought to Greece the knowledge of letters and the art of working in gold. Thebes is at our feet with the gloom of the terrible legends of Greek tragedy still lingering about it, the birthplace of Pindar, the nurse of Epaminondas and the Sacred Band.

And from out of the plain where 'Mars loved to dance,' rises the Muses' haunt, Helicon, by whose silver streams Corinna and Hesiod sang; while far away under the white ægis of those snow-capped mountains lies Chæronea and the Lion plain where with vain chivalry the Greeks strove to check Macedon first and afterwards Rome; Chæronea, where in the Martinmas summer of Greek civilisation Plutarch rose from the drear waste of a dying religion as the aftermath rises when the mowers think they have left the field bare.

Greek philosophy began and ended in scepticism: the first and the last word of Greek history was Faith.

Splendid thus in its death, like winter sunsets, the Greek religion passed away into the horror of night. For the Cimmerian darkness was at hand, and when the schools of Athens were closed and the statue of Athena broken, the Greek spirit passed from the gods and the history of its own land to the subtleties of defining the doctrine of the Trinity and the mystical attempts to bring Plato into harmony with Christ and to reconcile Gethsemane and the Sermon on the Mount with the Athenian prison and the discussion in the woods of Colonus. The Greek spirit slept for wellnigh a thousand years. When it woke again, like Antæus it had gathered strength from the earth where it lay; like Apollo it had lost none of its divinity through its long servitude.

In the history of Roman thought we nowhere find any of those characteristics of the Greek Illumination which I have pointed out are the necessary concomitants of the rise of historical criticism. The conservative respect for tradition which made the Roman people delight in the ritual and formulas of law, and is as apparent in their politics as in their religion, was fatal to any rise of that spirit of revolt against authority the importance of which, as a factor in intellectual progress, we have already seen.

The whitened tables of the Pontifices preserved carefully the records of the eclipses and other atmospherical phenomena, and what we call the art of verifying dates was known to them at an early time; but there was no spontaneous rise of physical science to suggest by its analogies of law and order a new method of research, nor any natural springing up of the questioning spirit of philosophy with its unification of all phenomena and all knowledge. At the very time when the whole tide of Eastern superstition was sweeping into the heart of the Capital the Senate banished the Greek philosophers from Rome. And of the three systems which did at length take some root in the city, those of Zeno and Epicurus were used merely as the rule for the ordering of life, while the dogmatic scepticism of Carneades, by its very principles, annihilated the possibility of argument and encouraged a perfect indifference to research.

Nor were the Romans ever fortunate enough like the Greeks to have to face the incubus of any dogmatic system of legends and myths, the immoralities and absurdities of which might excite a revolutionary outbreak of sceptical criticism. For the Roman religion became as it were crystallised and isolated from progress at an early period of its evolution. Their gods remained mere abstractions of commonplace virtues or uninteresting personifications of the useful things of life. The old primitive creed was indeed always upheld as a state institution on account of the enormous facilities it offered for cheating in politics, but as a spiritual system of belief it was unanimously rejected at a very early period both by the common people and the educated classes, for the sensible reason that it was so extremely dull. The former took refuge in the mystic sensualities of the worship of Isis, the latter in the Stoical rules of life. The Romans classified their gods carefully in their order of precedence, analysed their genealogies in the laborious spirit of modern heraldry, fenced them round with a ritual as intricate as their law, but never quite cared enough about them to believe in them. So it was of no account with them when the philosophers announced that Minerva was merely memory. She had never been much else. Nor did they protest when Lucretius dared to say of Ceres and of Liber that they were only the corn of the field and the fruit of the vine. For they had never mourned for the daughter of Demeter in the asphodel meadows of Sicily, nor traversed the glades of Cithæron with fawn-skin and with spear.

This brief sketch of the condition of Roman thought will serve to prepare us for the almost total want of scientific historical criticism which we shall discern in their literature, and has, besides, afforded fresh corroboration of the conditions essential to the rise of this spirit, and of the modes of thought which it reflects and in which it is always to be found. Roman historical composition had its origin in the pontifical college of ecclesiastical lawyers, and preserved to its close the uncritical spirit which characterised its fountain-head. It possessed from the outset a most voluminous collection of the materials of history, which, however, produced merely antiquarians, not historians. It is so hard to use facts, so easy to accumulate them.

Wearied of the dull monotony of the pontifical annals, which dwelt on little else but the rise and fall in provisions and the eclipses of the sun, Cato wrote out a history with his own hand for the instruction of his child, to which he gave the name of Origines, and before his time some aristocratic families had written histories in Greek much in the same spirit in which the Germans of the eighteenth century used French as the literary language. But the first regular Roman historian is Sallust. Between the extravagant eulogies passed on this author by the French (such as De Closset), and Dr. Mommsen's view of him as merely a political pamphleteer, it is perhaps difficult to reach the via media of unbiassed appreciation. He has, at any rate, the credit of being a purely rationalistic historian, perhaps the only one in Roman literature. Cicero had a good many qualifications for a scientific historian, and (as he usually did) thought very highly of his own powers. On passages of ancient legend, however, he is rather unsatisfactory, for while he is too sensible to believe them he is too patriotic to reject them. And this is really the attitude of Livy, who claims for early Roman legend a certain uncritical homage from the rest of the subject world. His view in his history is that it is not worth while to examine the truth of these stories.

In his hands the history of Rome unrolls before our eyes like some gorgeous tapestry, where victory succeeds victory, where triumph treads on the heels of triumph, and the line of heroes seems never to end. It is not till we pass behind the canvas and see the slight means by which the effect is produced that we apprehend the fact that like most picturesque writers Livy is an indifferent critic. As regards his attitude towards the credibility of early Roman history he is quite as conscious as we are of its mythical and unsound nature. He will not, for instance, decide whether the Horatii were Albans or Romans; who was the first dictator; how many tribunes there were, and the like. His method, as a rule, is merely to mention all the accounts and sometimes to decide in favour of the most probable, but usually not to decide at all. No canons of historical criticism will ever discover whether the Roman women interviewed the mother of Coriolanus of their own accord or at the suggestion of the senate; whether Remus was killed for jumping over his brother's wall or because they quarrelled about birds; whether the ambassadors found Cincinnatus ploughing or only mending a hedge. Livy suspends his judgment over these important facts and history when questioned on their truth is dumb. If he does select between two historians he chooses the one who is nearer to the facts he describes. But he is no critic, only a conscientious writer. It is mere vain waste to dwell on his critical powers, for they do not exist.

In the case of Tacitus imagination has taken the place of history. The past lives again in his pages, but through no laborious criticism; rather through a dramatic and psychological faculty which he specially possessed.

In the philosophy of history he has no belief. He can never make up his mind what to believe as regards God's government of the world. There is no method in him and none elsewhere in Roman literature.

Nations may not have missions but they certainly have functions. And the function of ancient Italy was not merely to give us what is statical in our institutions and rational in our law, but to blend into one elemental creed the spiritual aspirations of Aryan and of Semite. Italy was not a pioneer in intellectual progress, nor a motive power in the evolution of thought. The owl of the goddess of Wisdom traversed over the whole land and found nowhere a resting-place. The dove, which is the bird of Christ, flew straight to the city of Rome and the new reign began. It was the fashion of early Italian painters to represent in mediæval costume the soldiers who watched over the tomb of Christ, and this, which was the result of the frank anachronism of all true art, may serve to us as an allegory. For it was in vain that the Middle Ages strove to guard the buried spirit of progress. When the dawn of the Greek spirit arose, the sepulchre was empty, the grave-clothes laid aside. Humanity had risen from the dead.

The study of Greek, it has been well said, implies the birth of criticism, comparison and research. At the opening of that education of modern by ancient thought which we call the Renaissance, it was the words of Aristotle which sent Columbus sailing to the New World, while a fragment of Pythagorean astronomy set Copernicus thinking on that train of reasoning which has revolutionised the whole position of our planet in the universe. Then it was seen that the only meaning of progress is a return to Greek modes of thought. The monkish hymns which obscured the pages of Greek manuscripts were blotted out, the splendours of a new method were unfolded to the world, and out of the melancholy sea of mediævalism rose the free spirit of man in all that splendour of glad adolescence, when the bodily powers seem quickened by a new vitality, when the eye sees more clearly than its wont and the mind apprehends what was beforetime hidden from it. To herald the opening of the sixteenth century, from the little Venetian printing press came forth all the great authors of antiquity, each bearing on the title-page the words Ἄλδος ὁ Μανούτιος Ῥωμαῖος καὶ Φιλέλλην; words which may serve to remind us with what wondrous prescience Polybius saw the world's fate when he foretold the material sovereignty of Roman institutions and exemplified in himself the intellectual empire of Greece.

The course of the study of the spirit of historical criticism has not been a profitless investigation into modes and forms of thought now antiquated and of no account. The only spirit which is entirely removed from us is the mediæval; the Greek spirit is essentially modern. The introduction of the comparative method of research which has forced history to disclose its secrets belongs in a measure to us. Ours, too, is a more scientific knowledge of philology and the method of survival. Nor did the ancients know anything of the doctrine of averages or of crucial instances, both of which methods have proved of such importance in modern criticism, the one adding a most important proof of the statical elements of history, and exemplifying the influences of all physical surroundings on the life of man; the other, as in the single instance of the Moulin Quignon skull, serving to create a whole new science of prehistoric archæology and to bring us back to a time when man was coeval with the stone age, the mammoth and the woolly rhinoceros. But, except these, we have added no new canon or method to the science of historical criticism. Across the drear waste of a thousand years the Greek and the modern spirit join hands.

In the torch race which the Greek boys ran from the Cerameician field of death to the home of the goddess of Wisdom, not merely he who first reached the goal but he also who first started with the torch aflame received a prize. In the Lampadephoria of civilisation and free thought let us not forget to render due meed of honour to those who first lit that sacred flame, the increasing splendour of which lights our footsteps to the far-off divine event of the attainment of perfect truth.

THE ENGLISH RENAISSANCE OF ART

'The English Renaissance of Art' was delivered as a lecture for the first time in the Chickering Hall, New York, on January 9, 1882. A portion of it was reported in the *New York Tribune* on the following day and in other American papers subsequently. Since then this portion has been reprinted, more or less accurately, from time to time, in unauthorised editions.

There are in existence no less than four copies of the lecture, the earliest of which is entirely in the author's handwriting. The others are type-written and contain many corrections and additions made by the author in manuscript. These have all been collated and the text here given contains, as nearly as possible, the lecture in the original form as delivered by the author during his tour in the United States.

Among the many debts which we owe to the supreme æsthetic faculty of Goethe is that he was the first to teach us to define beauty in terms the most concrete possible, to realise it, I mean, always in its special manifestations. So, in the lecture which I have the honour to deliver before you, I will not try to give you any abstract definition of beauty—any such universal formula for it as was sought for by the philosophy of the eighteenth century—still less to communicate to you that which in its essence is incommunicable, the virtue by which a particular picture or poem affects us with a unique and special joy; but rather to point out to you the general ideas which characterise the great English Renaissance of Art in this century, to discover their source, as far as that is possible, and to estimate their future as far as that is possible.

I call it our English Renaissance because it is indeed a sort of new birth of the spirit of man, like the great Italian Renaissance of the fifteenth century, in its desire for a more gracious and comely way of life, its passion for physical beauty, its exclusive attention to form, its seeking for new subjects for poetry, new forms of art, new intellectual and imaginative enjoyments: and I call it our romantic movement because it is our most recent expression of beauty.

It has been described as a mere revival of Greek modes of thought, and again as a mere revival of mediæval feeling. Rather I would say that to these forms of the human spirit it has added whatever of artistic value the intricacy and complexity and experience of modern life can give: taking from the one its clearness of vision and its sustained calm, from the other its variety of expression and the mystery of its vision. For what, as Goethe said, is the study of the ancients but a return to the real world (for that is what they did); and what, said Mazzini, is mediævalism but individuality?

It is really from the union of Hellenism, in its breadth, its sanity of purpose, its calm possession of beauty, with the adventive, the intensified individualism, the passionate colour of the romantic spirit, that springs the art of the nineteenth century in England, as from the marriage of Faust and Helen of Troy sprang the beautiful boy Euphorion.

Such expressions as 'classical' and 'romantic' are, it is true, often apt to become the mere catchwords of schools. We must always remember that art has only one sentence to utter: there is for her only one high law, the law of form or harmony—yet between the classical and romantic spirit we may say that there lies this difference at least, that the one deals with the type and the other with the exception. In the work produced under the modern romantic spirit it is no longer the permanent, the essential truths of life that are treated of; it is the momentary situation of the one, the momentary aspect of the other that art seeks to render. In sculpture, which is the type of one spirit, the subject predominates over the situation; in painting, which is the type of the other, the situation predominates over the subject.

There are two spirits, then: the Hellenic spirit and the spirit of romance may be taken as forming the essential elements of our conscious intellectual tradition, of our permanent standard of taste. As regards their origin, in art as in politics there is but one origin for all revolutions, a desire on the part of man for a nobler form of life, for a freer method and opportunity of expression. Yet, I think that in estimating the sensuous and intellectual spirit which presides over our English Renaissance, any attempt to isolate it in any way from in the progress and movement and social life of the age that has produced it would be to rob it of its true vitality, possibly to mistake its true meaning. And in disengaging from the pursuits and passions of this crowded modern world those passions and pursuits which have to do with art and the love of art, we must take into account many great events of history which seem to be the most opposed to any such artistic feeling.

Alien then from any wild, political passion, or from the harsh voice of a rude people in revolt, as our English Renaissance must seem, in its passionate cult of pure beauty, its flawless devotion to form, its exclusive and sensitive nature, it is to the French Revolution that we must look for the most primary factor of its production, the first condition of its birth: that great Revolution of which we are all the children though the voices of some of us be often loud against it; that Revolution to which at a time when even such spirits as Coleridge and Wordsworth lost heart in England, noble messages of love blown across seas came from your young Republic.

It is true that our modern sense of the continuity of history has shown us that neither in politics nor in nature are there revolutions ever but evolutions only, and that the prelude to that wild storm which swept over France in 1789 and made every king in Europe tremble for his throne, was first sounded in literature years before the Bastille fell and the Palace was taken. The way for those red scenes by Seine and Loire was paved by that critical spirit of Germany and England which accustomed men to bring all things to the test of reason or utility or both, while the discontent of the people in the streets of Paris was the echo that followed the life of Emile and of Werther. For Rousseau, by silent lake and mountain, had called humanity back to the golden age that still lies before us and preached a return to nature, in passionate eloquence whose music still lingers about our keen northern air. And Goethe and Scott had brought romance back again from the prison she had lain in for so many centuries—and what is romance but humanity?

Yet in the womb of the Revolution itself, and in the storm and terror of that wild time, tendencies were hidden away that the artistic Renaissance bent to her own service when the time came—a scientific tendency first, which has borne in our own day a brood of somewhat noisy Titans, yet in the sphere of poetry has not been unproductive of good. I do not mean merely in its adding to enthusiasm that intellectual basis which in its strength, or that

74

more obvious influence about which Wordsworth was thinking when he said very nobly that poetry was merely the impassioned expression in the face of science, and that when science would put on a form of flesh and blood the poet would lend his divine spirit to aid the transfiguration. Nor do I dwell much on the great cosmical emotion and deep pantheism of science to which Shelley has given its first and Swinburne its latest glory of song, but rather on its influence on the artistic spirit in preserving that close observation and the sense of limitation as well as of clearness of vision which are the characteristics of the real artist.

The great and golden rule of art as well as of life, wrote William Blake, is that the more distinct, sharp and defined the boundary line, the more perfect is the work of art; and the less keen and sharp the greater is the evidence of weak imitation, plagiarism and bungling. 'Great inventors in all ages knew this—Michael Angelo and Albert Durer are known by this and by this alone'; and another time he wrote, with all the simple directness of nineteenth-century prose, 'to generalise is to be an idiot.'

And this love of definite conception, this clearness of vision, this artistic sense of limit, is the characteristic of all great work and poetry; of the vision of Homer as of the vision of Dante, of Keats and William Morris as of Chaucer and Theocritus. It lies at the base of all noble, realistic and romantic work as opposed to the colourless and empty abstractions of our own eighteenth-century poets and of the classical dramatists of France, or of the vague spiritualities of the German sentimental school: opposed, too, to that spirit of transcendentalism which also was root and flower itself of the great Revolution, underlying the impassioned contemplation of Wordsworth and giving wings and fire to the eagle-like flight of Shelley, and which in the sphere of philosophy, though displaced by the materialism and positiveness of our day, bequeathed two great schools of thought, the school of Newman to Oxford, the school of Emerson to America. Yet is this spirit of transcendentalism alien to the spirit of art. For the artist can accept no sphere of life in exchange for life itself. For him there is no escape from the bondage of the earth: there is not even the desire of escape.

He is indeed the only true realist: symbolism, which is the essence of the transcendental spirit, is alien to him. The metaphysical mind of Asia will create for itself the monstrous, many-breasted idol of Ephesus, but to the Greek, pure artist, that work is most instinct with spiritual life which conforms most clearly to the perfect facts of physical life.

'The storm of revolution,' as Andre Chenier said, 'blows out the torch of poetry.' It is not for some little time that the real influence of such a wild cataclysm of things is felt: at first the desire for equality seems to have produced personalities of more giant and Titan stature than the world had ever known before. Men heard the lyre of Byron and the legions of Napoleon; it was a period of measureless passions and of measureless despair; ambition, discontent, were the chords of life and art; the age was an age of revolt: a phase through which the human spirit must pass, but one in which it cannot rest. For the aim of culture is not rebellion but peace, the valley perilous where ignorant armies clash by night being no dwelling-place meet for her to whom the gods have assigned the fresh uplands and sunny heights and clear, untroubled air.

And soon that desire for perfection, which lay at the base of the Revolution, found in a young English poet its most complete and flawless realisation.

Phidias and the achievements of Greek art are foreshadowed in Homer: Dante prefigures for us the passion and colour and intensity of Italian painting: the modern love of landscape dates from Rousseau, and it is in Keats that one discerns the beginning of the artistic renaissance of England.

Byron was a rebel and Shelley a dreamer; but in the calmness and clearness of his vision, his perfect self-control, his unerring sense of beauty and his recognition of a separate realm for the imagination, Keats was the pure and serene artist, the forerunner of the pre-Raphaelite school, and so of the great romantic movement of which I am to speak.

Blake had indeed, before him, claimed for art a lofty, spiritual mission, and had striven to raise design to the ideal level of poetry and music, but the remoteness of his vision both in painting and poetry and the incompleteness of his technical powers had been adverse to any real influence. It is in Keats that the artistic spirit of this century first found its absolute incarnation.

And these pre-Raphaelites, what were they? If you ask nine-tenths of the British public what is the meaning of the word æsthetics, they will tell you it is the French for affectation or the German for a dado; and if you inquire about the pre-Raphaelites you will hear something about an eccentric lot of young men to whom a sort of divine crookedness and holy awkwardness in drawing were the chief objects of art. To know nothing about their great men is one of the necessary elements of English education.

As regards the pre-Raphaelites the story is simple enough. In the year 1847 a number of young men in London, poets and painters, passionate admirers of Keats all of them, formed the habit of meeting together for discussions on art, the result of such discussions being that the English Philistine public was roused suddenly from its ordinary apathy by hearing that there was in its midst a body of young men who had determined to revolutionise English painting and poetry. They called themselves the pre-Raphaelite Brotherhood.

In England, then as now, it was enough for a man to try and produce any serious beautiful work to lose all his rights as a citizen; and besides this, the pre-Raphaelite Brotherhood—among whom the names of Dante Rossetti, Holman Hunt and Millais will be familiar to you—had on their side three things that the English public never forgives: youth, power and enthusiasm.

Satire, always as sterile as it in shameful and as impotent as it is insolent, paid them that usual homage which mediocrity pays to genius—doing, here as always, infinite harm to the public, blinding them to what is beautiful, teaching them that irreverence which is the source of all vileness and narrowness of life, but harming the artist not at all, rather confirming him in the perfect rightness of his work and ambition. For to disagree with three-fourths of the British public on all points is one of the first elements of sanity, one of the deepest consolations in all moments of spiritual doubt.

As regards the ideas these young men brought to the regeneration of English art, we may see at the base of their artistic creations a desire for a deeper spiritual value to be given to art as well as a more decorative value.

Pre-Raphaelites they called themselves; not that they imitated the early Italian masters at all, but that in their work, as opposed to the facile abstractions of Raphael, they found a stronger realism of imagination, a more careful realism of technique, a vision at once more fervent and more vivid, an individuality more intimate and more intense.

For it is not enough that a work of art should conform to the æsthetic demands of its age: there must be also about it, if it is to affect us with any permanent delight, the impress of a distinct individuality, an individuality remote from that of ordinary men, and coming near to us only by virtue of a certain newness and wonder in the work, and through channels whose very strangeness makes us more ready to give them welcome.

La personnalité, said one of the greatest of modern French critics, voilà ce qui nous sauvera.

But above all things was it a return to Nature—that formula which seems to suit so many and such diverse movements: they would draw and paint nothing but what they saw, they would try and imagine things as they really happened. Later there came to the old house by Blackfriars Bridge, where this young brotherhood used to meet and work, two young men from Oxford, Edward Burne-Jones and William Morris—the latter substituting for the simpler realism of the early days a more exquisite spirit of choice, a more faultless devotion to beauty, a more intense seeking for perfection: a master of all exquisite design and of all spiritual vision. It is of the school of Florence rather than of that of Venice that he is kinsman, feeling that the close imitation of Nature is a disturbing element in imaginative art. The visible aspect of modern life disturbs him not; rather is it for him to render eternal all that is beautiful in Greek, Italian, and Celtic legend. To Morris we owe poetry whose perfect precision and clearness of word and vision has not been excelled in the literature of our country, and by the revival of the decorative arts he has given to our individualised romantic movement the social idea and the social factor also.

But the revolution accomplished by this clique of young men, with Ruskin's faultless and fervent eloquence to help them, was not one of ideas merely but of execution, not one of conceptions but of creations.

For the great eras in the history of the development of all the arts have been eras not of increased feeling or enthusiasm in feeling for art, but of new technical improvements primarily and specially. The discovery of marble quarries in the purple ravines of Pentelicus and on the little low-lying hills of the island of Paros gave to the Greeks the opportunity for that intensified vitality of action, that more sensuous and simple humanism, to which the Egyptian sculptor working laboriously in the hard porphyry and rose-coloured granite of the desert could not attain. The splendour of the Venetian school began with the introduction of the new oil medium for painting. The progress in modern music has been due to the invention of new instruments entirely, and in no way to an increased consciousness on the part of the musician of any wider social aim. The critic may try and trace the deferred resolutions of Beethoven [124] to some sense of the incompleteness of the modern intellectual spirit, but the artist would have answered, as one of them did afterwards, 'Let them pick out the fifths and leave us at peace.'

And so it is in poetry also: all this love of curious French metres like the Ballade, the Villanelle, the Rondel; all this increased value laid on elaborate alliterations, and on curious words and refrains, such as you will find in Dante Rossetti and Swinburne, is merely the attempt to perfect flute and viol and trumpet through which the spirit of the age and the lips of the poet may blow the music of their many messages.

And so it has been with this romantic movement of ours: it is a reaction against the empty conventional workmanship, the lax execution of previous poetry and painting, showing itself in the work of such men as Rossetti and Burne-Jones by a far greater splendour of colour, a far more intricate wonder of design than English imaginative art has shown before. In Rossetti's poetry and the poetry of Morris, Swinburne and Tennyson a perfect precision and choice of language, a style flawless and fearless, a seeking for all sweet and precious melodies and a sustaining consciousness of the musical value of each word are opposed to that value which is merely intellectual. In this respect they are one with the romantic movement of France of which not the least characteristic note was struck by Théophile Gautier's advice to the young poet to read his dictionary every day, as being the only book worth a poet's reading.

While, then, the material of workmanship is being thus elaborated and discovered to have in itself incommunicable and eternal qualities of its own, qualities entirely satisfying to the poetic sense and not needing for their æsthetic effect any lofty intellectual vision, any deep criticism of life or even any passionate human emotion at all, the spirit and the method of the poet's working—what people call his inspiration—have not escaped the controlling influence of the artistic spirit. Not that the imagination has lost its wings, but we have accustomed ourselves to count their innumerable pulsations, to estimate their limitless strength, to govern their ungovernable freedom.

To the Greeks this problem of the conditions of poetic production, and the places occupied by either spontaneity or self-consciousness in any artistic work, had a peculiar fascination. We find it in the mysticism of Plato and in the rationalism of Aristotle. We find it later in the Italian Renaissance agitating the minds of such men as Leonardo da Vinci. Schiller tried to adjust the balance between form and feeling, and Goethe to estimate the position of self-consciousness in art. Wordsworth's definition of poetry as 'emotion remembered in tranquillity' may be taken as an analysis of one of the stages through which all imaginative work has to pass; and in Keats's longing to be 'able to compose without this fever' (I quote from one of his letters), his desire to substitute for poetic ardour 'a more thoughtful and quiet power,' we may discern the most important moment in the evolution of that artistic life. The question made an early and strange appearance in your literature too; and I need not remind you how deeply the young poets of the French romantic movement were excited and stirred by Edgar Allan Poe's analysis of the workings of his own imagination in the creating of that supreme imaginative work which we know by the name of The Raven.

In the last century, when the intellectual and didactic element had intruded to such an extent into the kingdom which belongs to poetry, it was against the claims of the understanding that an artist like Goethe had to protest. 'The more incomprehensible to the understanding a poem is the better for it,' he said once, asserting the complete supremacy of the imagination in poetry as of reason in prose. But in this century it is rather against the claims of the emotional faculties, the claims of mere sentiment and feeling, that the artist must react. The simple utterance of joy is not poetry any more than a mere personal cry of pain, and the real experiences of the artist are always those which do not find their direct expression but are gathered up and absorbed into some artistic form which seems, from such real experiences, to be the farthest removed and the most alien.

'The heart contains passion but the imagination alone contains poetry,' says Charles Baudelaire. This too was the lesson that Théophile Gautier, most subtle of all modern critics, most fascinating of all modern poets, was never tired of teaching—'Everybody is affected by a sunrise or a sunset.' The absolute distinction of the artist is not his capacity to feel nature so much as his power of rendering it. The entire subordination of all intellectual and emotional faculties to the vital and informing poetic principle is the surest sign of the strength of our Renaissance.

We have seen the artistic spirit working, first in the delightful and technical sphere of language, the sphere of expression as opposed to subject, then controlling the imagination of the poet in dealing with his subject. And now I would point out to you its operation in the choice of subject. The recognition of a separate realm for the artist, a consciousness of the absolute difference between the world of art and the world of real fact, between classic grace and absolute reality, forms not merely the essential element of any æsthetic charm but is the characteristic of all great imaginative work and of all great eras of artistic creation—of the age of Phidias as of the age of Michael Angelo, of the age of Sophocles as of the age of Goethe.

Art never harms itself by keeping aloof from the social problems of the day: rather, by so doing, it more completely realises for us that which we desire. For to most of us the real life is the life we do not lead, and thus, remaining more true to the essence of its own perfection, more jealous of its own unattainable beauty, is less likely to forget form in feeling or to accept the passion of creation as any substitute for the beauty of the created thing.

The artist is indeed the child of his own age, but the present will not be to him a whit more real than the past; for, like the philosopher of the Platonic vision, the poet is the spectator of all time and of all existence. For him no form is obsolete, no subject out of date; rather, whatever of life and passion the world has known, in desert of Judæa or in Arcadian valley, by the rivers of Troy or the rivers of Damascus, in the crowded and hideous streets of a modern city or by the pleasant ways of Camelot—all lies before him like an open scroll, all is still instinct with beautiful life. He will take of it what is salutary for his own spirit, no more; choosing some facts and rejecting others with the calm artistic control of one who is in possession of the secret of beauty.

There is indeed a poetical attitude to be adopted towards all things, but all things are not fit subjects for poetry. Into the secure and sacred house of Beauty the true artist will admit nothing that is harsh or disturbing, nothing that gives pain, nothing that is debatable, nothing about which men argue. He can steep himself, if he wishes, in the discussion of all the social problems of his day, poor-laws and local taxation, free trade and bimetallic currency, and the like; but when he writes on these subjects it will be, as Milton nobly expressed it, with his left hand, in prose and not in verse, in a pamphlet and not in a lyric. This exquisite spirit of artistic choice was not in Byron: Wordsworth had it not. In the work of both these men there is much that we have to reject, much that does not give us that sense of calm and perfect repose which should be the effect of all fine, imaginative work. But in Keats it seemed to have been incarnate, and in his lovely Ode on a Grecian Urn it found its most secure and faultless expression; in the pageant of the Earthly Paradise and the knights and ladies of Burne-Jones it is the one dominant note.

It is to no avail that the Muse of Poetry be called, even by such a clarion note as Whitman's, to migrate from Greece and Ionia and to placard REMOVED and TO LET on the rocks of the snowy Parnassus. Calliope's call is not yet closed, nor are the epics of Asia ended; the Sphinx is not yet silent, nor the fountain of Castaly dry. For art is very life itself and knows nothing of death; she is absolute truth and takes no care of fact; she sees (as I remember Mr. Swinburne insisting on at dinner) that Achilles is even now more actual and real than Wellington, not merely more noble and interesting as a type and figure but more positive and real.

Literature must rest always on a principle, and temporal considerations are no principle at all. For to the poet all times and places are one; the stuff he deals with is eternal and eternally the same: no theme is inept, no past or present preferable. The steam whistle will not affright him nor the flutes of Arcadia weary him: for him there is but one time, the artistic moment; but one law, the law of form; but one land, the land of Beauty—a land removed indeed from the real world and yet more sensuous because more enduring; calm, yet with that calm which dwells in the faces of the Greek statues, the calm which comes not from the rejection but from the absorption of passion, the calm which despair and sorrow cannot disturb but intensify only. And so it comes that he who seems to stand most remote from his age is he who mirrors it best, because he has stripped life of what is accidental and transitory, stripped it of that 'mist of familiarity which makes life obscure to us.'

Those strange, wild-eyed sibyls fixed eternally in the whirlwind of ecstasy, those mighty-limbed and Titan prophets, labouring with the secret of the earth and the burden of mystery, that guard and glorify the chapel of Pope Sixtus at Rome—do they not tell us more of the real spirit of the Italian Renaissance, of the dream of Savonarola and of the sin of Borgia, than all the brawling boors and cooking women of Dutch art can teach us of the real spirit of the history of Holland?

And so in our own day, also, the two most vital tendencies of the nineteenth century—the democratic and pantheistic tendency and the tendency to value life for the sake of art—found their most complete and perfect utterance in the poetry of Shelley and Keats who, to the blind eyes of their own time, seemed to be as wanderers in the wilderness, preachers of vague or unreal things. And I remember once, in talking to Mr. Burne-Jones about modern science, his saying to me, 'the more materialistic science becomes, the more angels shall I paint: their wings are my protest in favour of the immortality of the soul.'

But these are the intellectual speculations that underlie art. Where in the arts themselves are we to find that breadth of human sympathy which is the condition of all noble work; where in the arts are we to look for what Mazzini would call the social ideas as opposed to the merely personal ideas? By virtue of what claim do I demand for the artist the love and loyalty of the men and women of the world? I think I can answer that.

Whatever spiritual message an artist brings to his aid is a matter for his own soul. He may bring judgment like Michael Angelo or peace like Angelico; he may come with mourning like the great Athenian or with mirth like the singer of Sicily; nor is it for us to do aught but accept his teaching, knowing that we cannot smite the bitter lips of Leopardi into laughter or burden with our discontent Goethe's serene calm. But for warrant of its truth such message must have the flame of eloquence in the lips that speak it, splendour and glory in the vision that is its witness, being justified by one thing only—the flawless beauty and perfect form of its expression: this indeed being the social idea, being the meaning of joy in art.

Not laughter where none should laugh, nor the calling of peace where there is no peace; not in painting the subject ever, but the pictorial charm only, the wonder of its colour, the satisfying beauty of its design.

You have most of you seen, probably, that great masterpiece of Rubens which hangs in the gallery of Brussels, that swift and wonderful pageant of horse and rider arrested in its most exquisite and fiery moment when the winds are caught in crimson banner and the air lit by the gleam of armour and the flash of plume. Well, that is joy in art, though that golden hillside be trodden by the wounded feet of Christ and it is for the death of the Son of Man that that gorgeous cavalcade is passing.

But this restless modern intellectual spirit of ours is not receptive enough of the sensuous element of art; and so the real influence of the arts is hidden from many of us: only a few, escaping from the tyranny of the soul, have learned the secret of those high hours when thought is not.

And this indeed is the reason of the influence which Eastern art is having on us in Europe, and of the fascination of all Japanese work. While the Western world has been laying on art the intolerable burden of its own intellectual doubts and the spiritual tragedy of its own sorrows, the East has always kept true to art's primary and pictorial conditions.

In judging of a beautiful statue the æsthetic faculty is absolutely and completely gratified by the splendid curves of those marble lips that are dumb to our complaint, the noble modelling of those limbs that are powerless to help us. In its primary aspect a painting has no more spiritual message or meaning than an exquisite fragment of Venetian glass or a blue tile from the wall of Damascus: it is a beautifully coloured surface, nothing more. The channels by which all noble imaginative work in painting should touch, and do touch the soul, are not those of the truths of life, nor metaphysical truths. But that pictorial charm which does not depend on any literary reminiscence for its effect on the one hand, nor is yet a mere result of communicable technical skill on the other, comes of a certain inventive and creative handling of colour. Nearly always in Dutch painting and often in the works of Giorgione or Titian, it is entirely independent of anything definitely poetical in the subject, a kind of form and choice in workmanship which is itself entirely satisfying, and is (as the Greeks would say) an end in itself.

And so in poetry too, the real poetical quality, the joy of poetry, comes never from the subject but from an inventive handling of rhythmical language, from what Keats called the 'sensuous life of verse.' The element of song in the singing accompanied by the profound joy of motion, is so sweet that, while the incomplete lives of ordinary men bring no healing power with them, the thorn-crown of the poet will blossom into roses for our pleasure; for our delight his despair will gild its own thorns, and his pain, like Adonis, be beautiful in its agony; and when the poet's heart breaks it will break in music.

And health in art—what is that? It has nothing to do with a sane criticism of life. There is more health in Baudelaire than there is in [Kingsley]. Health is the artist's recognition of the limitations of the form in which he works. It is the honour and the homage which he gives to the material he uses—whether it be language with its glories, or marble or pigment with their glories—knowing that the true brotherhood of the arts consists not in their borrowing one another's method, but in their producing, each of them by its own individual means, each of them by keeping its objective limits, the same unique artistic delight. The delight is like that given to us by music—for music is the art in which form and matter are always one, the art whose subject cannot be separated from the method of its expression, the art which most completely realises the artistic ideal, and is the condition to which all the other arts are constantly aspiring.

And criticism—what place is that to have in our culture? Well, I think that the first duty of an art critic is to hold his tongue at all times, and upon all subjects: C'est un grand avantage de n'avoir rien fait, mais il ne faut pas en abuser.

It is only through the mystery of creation that one can gain any knowledge of the quality of created things. You have listened to Patience for a hundred nights and you have heard me for one only. It will make, no doubt, that satire more piquant by knowing something about the subject of it, but you must not judge of æstheticism by the satire of Mr. Gilbert. As little should you judge of the strength and splendour of sun or sea by the dust that dances in the beam, or the bubble that breaks on the wave, as take your critic for any sane test of art. For the artists, like the Greek gods, are revealed only to one another, as Emerson says somewhere; their real value and place time only can show. In this respect also omnipotence is with the ages. The true critic addresses not the artist ever but the public only. His work lies with them. Art can never have any other claim but her own perfection: it is for the critic to create for art the social aim, too, by teaching the people the spirit in which they are to approach all artistic work, the love they are to give it, the lesson they are to draw from it.

All these appeals to art to set herself more in harmony with modern progress and civilisation, and to make herself the mouthpiece for the voice of humanity, these appeals to art 'to have a mission,' are appeals which should be made to the public. The art which has fulfilled the conditions of beauty has fulfilled all conditions: it is for the critic to teach the people how to find in the calm of such art the highest expression of their own most stormy passions. 'I have no reverence,' said Keats, 'for the public, nor for anything in existence but the Eternal Being, the memory of great men and the principle of Beauty.'

Such then is the principle which I believe to be guiding and underlying our English Renaissance, a Renaissance many-sided and wonderful, productive of strong ambitions and lofty personalities, yet for all its splendid achievements in poetry and in the decorative arts and in painting, for all the increased comeliness and grace of dress, and the furniture of houses and the like, not complete. For there can be no great sculpture without a beautiful national life, and the commercial spirit of England has killed that; no great drama without a noble national life, and the commercial spirit of England has killed that too.

It is not that the flawless serenity of marble cannot bear the burden of the modern intellectual spirit, or become instinct with the fire of romantic passion—the tomb of Duke Lorenzo and the chapel of the Medici show us that—but it is that, as Théophile Gautier used to say, the visible world is dead, le monde visible a disparu.

Nor is it again that the novel has killed the play, as some critics would persuade us—the romantic movement of France shows us that. The work of Balzac and of Hugo grew up side by side together; nay, more, were complementary to each other, though neither of them saw it. While all other forms of poetry may flourish in an ignoble age, the splendid individualism of the lyrist, fed by its own passion, and lit by its own power, may pass as a pillar of fire as well across the desert as across places that are pleasant. It is none the less glorious though no man follow it—nay, by the greater sublimity of its loneliness it may be quickened into loftier utterance and intensified into clearer song. From the mean squalor of the sordid life that limits him, the dreamer or the idyllist may soar on poesy's viewless wings, may traverse with fawn-skin and spear the moonlit heights of Cithæron though Faun and Bassarid dance there no more. Like Keats he may wander through the old-world forests of Latmos, or stand like Morris on the galley's deck with the Viking when king and galley have long since passed away. But the drama is the meeting-place of art and life; it deals, as Mazzini said, not merely with man, but with social man, with man in his relation to God and to Humanity. It is the product of a period of great national united energy; it is impossible without a noble public, and belongs to such ages as the age of Elizabeth in London and of Pericles at Athens; it is part of such lofty moral and spiritual ardour as came to Greek after the defeat of the Persian fleet, and to Englishman after the wreck of the Armada of Spain.

Shelley felt how incomplete our movement was in this respect, and has shown in one great tragedy by what terror and pity he would have purified our age; but in spite of The Cenci the drama is one of the artistic forms through which the genius of the England of this century seeks in vain to find outlet and expression. He has had no worthy imitators.

It is rather, perhaps, to you that we should turn to complete and perfect this great movement of ours, for there is something Hellenic in your air and world, something that has a quicker breath of the joy and power of Elizabeth's England about it than our ancient civilisation can give us. For you, at least, are young; 'no hungry generations tread you down,' and the past does not weary you with the intolerable burden of its memories nor mock you with the ruins of a beauty, the secret of whose creation you have lost. That very absence of tradition, which Mr. Ruskin thought would rob your rivers of their laughter and your flowers of their light, may be rather the source of your freedom and your strength.

To speak in literature with the perfect rectitude and insouciance of the movements of animals, and the unimpeachableness of the sentiment of trees in the woods and grass by the roadside, has been defined by one of your poets as a flawless triumph of art. It is a triumph which you above all nations may be destined to achieve. For the voices that have their dwelling in sea and mountain are not the chosen music of Liberty only; other messages are there in the wonder of wind-swept height and the majesty of silent deep—messages that, if you will but listen to them, may yield you the splendour of some new imagination, the marvel of some new beauty.

'I foresee,' said Goethe, 'the dawn of a new literature which all people may claim as their own, for all have contributed to its foundation.' If, then, this is so, and if the materials for a civilisation as great as that of Europe lie all around you, what profit, you will ask me, will all this study of our poets and painters be to you? I might answer that the intellect can be engaged without direct didactic object on an artistic and historical problem; that the demand of the intellect is merely to feel itself alive; that nothing which has ever interested men or women can cease to be a fit subject for culture.

I might remind you of what all Europe owes to the sorrow of a single Florentine in exile at Verona, or to the love of Petrarch by that little well in Southern France; nay, more, how even in this dull, materialistic age the simple expression of an old man's simple life, passed away from the clamour of great cities amid the lakes and misty hills of Cumberland, has opened out for England treasures of new joy compared with which the treasures of her luxury are as barren as the sea which she has made her highway, and as bitter as the fire which she would make her slave.

But I think it will bring you something besides this, something that is the knowledge of real strength in art: not that you should imitate the works of these men; but their artistic spirit, their artistic attitude, I think you should absorb that.

For in nations, as in individuals, if the passion for creation be not accompanied by the critical, the æsthetic faculty also, it will be sure to waste its strength aimlessly, failing perhaps in the artistic spirit of choice, or in the mistaking of feeling for form, or in the following of false ideals.

For the various spiritual forms of the imagination have a natural affinity with certain sensuous forms of art—and to discern the qualities of each art, to intensify as well its limitations as its powers of expression, is one of the aims that culture sets before us. It is not an increased moral sense, an increased moral supervision that your literature needs. Indeed, one should never talk of a moral or an immoral poem—poems are either well written or badly written, that is all. And, indeed, any element of morals or implied reference to a standard of good or evil in art is often a sign of a certain incompleteness of vision, often a note of discord in the harmony of an imaginative creation; for all good work aims at a purely artistic effect. 'We must be careful,' said Goethe, 'not to be always looking for culture merely in what is obviously moral. Everything that is great promotes civilisation as soon as we are aware of it.'

But, as in your cities so in your literature, it is a permanent canon and standard of taste, an increased sensibility to beauty (if I may say so) that is lacking. All noble work is not national merely, but universal. The political independence of a nation must not be confused with any intellectual isolation. The spiritual freedom, indeed, your own generous lives and liberal air will give you. From us you will learn the classical restraint of form.

For all great art is delicate art, roughness having very little to do with strength, and harshness very little to do with power. 'The artist,' as Mr. Swinburne says, 'must be perfectly articulate.'

This limitation is for the artist perfect freedom: it is at once the origin and the sign of his strength. So that all the supreme masters of style—Dante, Sophocles, Shakespeare—are the supreme masters of spiritual and intellectual vision also.

Love art for its own sake, and then all things that you need will be added to you.

This devotion to beauty and to the creation of beautiful things is the test of all great civilised nations. Philosophy may teach us to bear with equanimity the misfortunes of our neighbours, and science resolve the moral sense into a secretion of sugar, but art is what makes the life of each citizen a sacrament and not a speculation, art is what makes the life of the whole race immortal.

For beauty is the only thing that time cannot harm. Philosophies fall away like sand, and creeds follow one another like the withered leaves of autumn; but what is beautiful is a joy for all seasons and a possession for all eternity.

Wars and the clash of armies and the meeting of men in battle by trampled field or leaguered city, and the rising of nations there must always be. But I think that art, by creating a common intellectual atmosphere between all countries, might—if it could not overshadow the world with the silver wings of peace—at least make men such brothers that they would not go out to slay one another for the whim or folly of some king or minister, as they do in Europe. Fraternity would come no more with the hands of Cain, nor Liberty betray freedom with the kiss of Anarchy; for national hatreds are always strongest where culture is lowest.

'How could I?' said Goethe, when reproached for not writing like Korner against the French. 'How could I, to whom barbarism and culture alone are of importance, hate a nation which is among the most cultivated of the earth, a nation to which I owe a great part of my own cultivation?'

Mighty empires, too, there must always be as long as personal ambition and the spirit of the age are one, but art at least is the only empire which a nation's enemies cannot take from her by conquest, but which is taken by submission only. The sovereignty of Greece and Rome is not yet passed away, though the gods of the one be dead and the eagles of the other tired.

And we in our Renaissance are seeking to create a sovereignty that will still be England's when her yellow leopards have grown weary of wars and the rose of her shield is crimsoned no more with the blood of battle; and you, too, absorbing into the generous heart of a great people this pervading artistic spirit, will create for yourselves such riches as you have never yet created, though your land be a network of railways and your cities the harbours for the galleys of the world.

I know, indeed, that the divine natural prescience of beauty which is the inalienable inheritance of Greek and Italian is not our inheritance. For such an informing and presiding spirit of art to shield us from all harsh and alien influences, we of the Northern races must turn rather to that strained self-consciousness of our age which, as it is the key-note of all our romantic art, must be the source of all or nearly all our culture. I mean that intellectual curiosity of the nineteenth century which is always looking for the secret of the life that still lingers round old and bygone forms of culture. It takes from each what is serviceable for the modern spirit—from Athens its wonder without its worship, from Venice its splendour without its sin. The same spirit is always analysing its own strength and its own weakness, counting what it owes to East and to West, to the olive-trees of Colonus and to the palm-trees of Lebanon, to Gethsemane and to the garden of Proserpine.

And yet the truths of art cannot be taught: they are revealed only, revealed to natures which have made themselves receptive of all beautiful impressions by the study and worship of all beautiful things. And hence the enormous importance given to the decorative arts in our English Renaissance; hence all that marvel of design that comes from the hand of Edward Burne-Jones, all that weaving of tapestry and staining of glass, that beautiful working in clay and metal and wood which we owe to William Morris, the greatest handicraftsman we have had in England since the fourteenth century.

So, in years to come there will be nothing in any man's house which has not given delight to its maker and does not give delight to its user. The children, like the children of Plato's perfect city, will grow up 'in a simple atmosphere of all fair things'—I quote from the passage in the Republic—'a simple atmosphere of all fair things, where beauty, which is the spirit of art, will come on eye and ear like a fresh breath of wind that brings health from a clear upland, and insensibly and gradually draw the child's soul into harmony with all knowledge and all wisdom, so that he will love what is beautiful and good, and hate what is evil and ugly (for they always go together) long before he knows the reason why; and then when reason comes will kiss her on the cheek as a friend.'

That is what Plato thought decorative art could do for a nation, feeling that the secret not of philosophy merely but of all gracious existence might be externally hidden from any one whose youth had been passed in uncomely and vulgar surroundings, and that the beauty of form and colour even, as he says, in the meanest vessels of the house, will find its way into the inmost places of the soul and lead the boy naturally to look for that divine harmony of spiritual life of which art was to him the material symbol and warrant.

Prelude indeed to all knowledge and all wisdom will this love of beautiful things be for us; yet there are times when wisdom becomes a burden and knowledge is one with sorrow: for as every body has its shadow so every soul has its scepticism. In such dread moments of discord and despair where should we, of this torn and troubled age, turn our steps if not to that secure house of beauty where there is always a little forgetfulness, always a great joy; to that città divina, as the old Italian heresy called it, the divine city where one can stand, though only for a brief moment, apart from the division and terror of the world and the choice of the world too?

This is that consolation des arts which is the key-note of Gautier's poetry, the secret of modern life foreshadowed—as indeed what in our century is not?—by Goethe. You remember what he said to the German people: 'Only have the courage,' he said, 'to give yourselves up to your impressions, allow yourselves to be delighted, moved, elevated, nay instructed, inspired for something great.' The courage to give yourselves up to your impressions: yes, that is the secret of the artistic life—for while art has been defined as an escape from the tyranny of the senses, it is an escape rather from the tyranny of the soul. But only to those who worship her above all things does she ever reveal her true treasure: else will she be as powerless to aid you as the mutilated Venus of the Louvre was before the romantic but sceptical nature of Heine.

And indeed I think it would be impossible to overrate the gain that might follow if we had about us only what gave pleasure to the maker of it and gives pleasure to its user, that being the simplest of all rules about decoration. One thing, at least, I think it would do for us: there is no surer test of a great country than how near it stands to its own poets; but between the singers of our day and the workers to whom they would sing there seems to be an ever-widening and dividing chasm, a chasm which slander and mockery cannot traverse, but which is spanned by the luminous wings of love.

And of such love I think that the abiding presence in our houses of noble imaginative work would be the surest seed and preparation. I do not mean merely as regards that direct literary expression of art by which, from the little red-and-black cruse of oil or wine, a Greek boy could learn of the lionlike splendour of Achilles, of the strength of Hector and the beauty of Paris and the wonder of Helen, long before he stood and listened in crowded market-place or in theatre of marble; or by which an Italian child of the fifteenth century could know of the chastity of Lucrece and the death of Camilla from carven doorway and from painted chest. For the good we get from art is not what we learn from it; it is what we become through it. Its real influence will be in giving the mind that enthusiasm which is the secret of Hellenism, accustoming it to demand from art all that art can do in rearranging the facts of common life for us—whether it be by giving the most spiritual interpretation of one's own moments of highest passion or the most sensuous expression of those thoughts that are the farthest removed from sense; in accustoming it to love the things of the imagination for their own sake, and to desire beauty and grace in all things. For he who does not love art in all things does not love it at all, and he who does not need art in all things does not need it at all.

I will not dwell here on what I am sure has delighted you all in our great Gothic cathedrals. I mean how the artist of that time, handicraftsman himself in stone or glass, found the best motives for his art, always ready for his hand and always beautiful, in the daily work of the artificers he saw around him—as in those lovely windows of Chartres—where the dyer dips in the vat and the potter sits at the wheel, and the weaver stands at the loom: real manufacturers these, workers with the hand, and entirely delightful to look at, not like the smug and vapid shopman of our time, who knows nothing of the web or vase he sells, except that he is charging you double its value and thinking you a fool for buying it. Nor can I but just note, in passing, the immense influence the decorative work of Greece and Italy had on its artists, the one teaching the sculptor that restraining influence of design which is the glory of the Parthenon, the other keeping painting always true to its primary, pictorial condition of noble colour which is the secret of the school of Venice; for I wish rather, in this lecture at least, to dwell on the effect that decorative art has on human life—on its social not its purely artistic effect.

There are two kinds of men in the world, two great creeds, two different forms of natures: men to whom the end of life is action, and men to whom the end of life is thought. As regards the latter, who seek for experience itself and not for the fruits of experience, who must burn always with one of the passions of this fiery-coloured world, who find life interesting not for its secret but for its situations, for its pulsations and not for its purpose; the passion for beauty engendered by the decorative arts will be to them more satisfying than any political or religious enthusiasm, any enthusiasm for humanity, any ecstasy or sorrow for love. For art comes to one professing primarily to give nothing but the highest quality to one's moments, and for those moments' sake. So far for those to whom the end of life is thought.

As regards the others, who hold that life is inseparable from labour, to them should this movement be specially dear: for, if our days are barren without industry, industry without art is barbarism.

Hewers of wood and drawers of water there must be always indeed among us. Our modern machinery has not much lightened the labour of man after all: but at least let the pitcher that stands by the well be beautiful and surely the labour of the day will be lightened: let the wood be made receptive of some lovely form, some gracious design, and there will come no longer discontent but joy to the toiler. For what is decoration but the worker's expression of joy in his work? And not joy merely—that is a great thing yet not enough—but that opportunity of expressing his own individuality which, as it is the essence of all life, is the source of all art. 'I have tried,' I remember William Morris saying to me once, 'I have tried to make each of my workers an artist, and when I say an artist I mean a man.' For the worker then, handicraftsman of whatever kind he is, art is no longer to be a purple robe woven by a slave and thrown over the whitened body of a leprous king to hide and to adorn the sin of his luxury, but rather the beautiful and noble expression of a life that has in it something beautiful and noble.

And so you must seek out your workman and give him, as far as possible, the right surroundings, for remember that the real test and virtue of a workman is not his earnestness nor his industry even, but his power of design merely; and that 'design is not the offspring of idle fancy: it is the studied result of accumulative observation and delightful habit.' All the teaching in the world is of no avail if you do not surround your workman with happy influences and with beautiful things. It is impossible for him to have right ideas about colour unless he sees the lovely colours of Nature unspoiled; impossible for him to supply beautiful incident and action unless he sees beautiful incident and action in the world about him.

For to cultivate sympathy you must be among living things and thinking about them, and to cultivate admiration you must be among beautiful things and looking at them. 'The steel of Toledo and the silk of Genoa did but give strength to oppression and lustre to pride,' as Mr. Ruskin says; let it be for you to create an art that is made by the hands of the people for the joy of the people, to please the hearts of the people, too; an art that will be your expression of your delight in life. There is nothing 'in common life too mean, in common things too trivial to be ennobled by your touch'; nothing in life that art cannot sanctify.

You have heard, I think, a few of you, of two flowers connected with the æsthetic movement in England, and said (I assure you, erroneously) to be the food of some æsthetic young men. Well, let me tell you that the reason we love the lily and the sunflower, in spite of what Mr. Gilbert may tell you, is not for any vegetable fashion at all. It is because these two lovely flowers are in England the two most perfect models of design, the most naturally adapted for decorative art—the gaudy leonine beauty of the one and the precious loveliness of the other giving to the artist the most entire and perfect joy. And so with you: let there be no flower in your meadows that does not wreathe its tendrils around your pillows, no little leaf in your Titan forests that does not lend its form to design, no curving spray of wild rose or brier that does not live for ever in carven arch or window or marble, no bird in your air that is not giving the iridescent wonder of its colour, the exquisite curves of its wings in flight, to make more precious the preciousness of simple adornment.

We spend our days, each one of us, in looking for the secret of life. Well, the secret of life is in art.

HOUSE DECORATION

A lecture delivered in America during Wilde's tour in 1882. It was announced as a lecture on 'The Practical Application of the Principles of Æsthetic Theory to Exterior and Interior House Decoration, With Observations upon Dress and Personal Ornaments.' The earliest date on which it is known to have been given is May 11, 1882.

In my last lecture I gave you something of the history of Art in England. I sought to trace the influence of the French Revolution upon its development. I said something of the song of Keats and the school of the pre-Raphaelites. But I do not want to shelter the movement, which I have called the English Renaissance, under any palladium however noble, or any name however revered. The roots of it have, indeed, to be sought for in things that have long passed away, and not, as some suppose, in the fancy of a few young men—although I am not altogether sure that there is anything much better than the fancy of a few young men.

When I appeared before you on a previous occasion, I had seen nothing of American art save the Doric columns and Corinthian chimney-pots visible on your Broadway and Fifth Avenue. Since then, I have been through your country to some fifty or sixty different cities, I think. I find that what your people need is not so much high imaginative art but that which hallows the vessels of everyday use. I suppose that the poet will sing and the artist will paint regardless whether the world praises or blames. He has his own world and is independent of his fellow-men. But the handicraftsman is dependent on your pleasure and opinion. He needs your encouragement and he must have beautiful surroundings. Your people love art but do not sufficiently honour the handicraftsman. Of course, those millionaires who can pillage Europe for their pleasure need have no care to encourage such; but I speak for those whose desire for beautiful things is larger than their means. I find that one great trouble all over is that your workmen are not given to noble designs. You cannot be indifferent to this, because Art is not something which you can take or leave. It is a necessity of human life.

And what is the meaning of this beautiful decoration which we call art? In the first place, it means value to the workman and it means the pleasure which he must necessarily take in making a beautiful thing. The mark of all good art is not that the thing done is done exactly or finely, for machinery may do as much, but that it is worked out with the head and the workman's heart. I cannot impress the point too frequently that beautiful and rational designs are necessary in all work. I did not imagine, until I went into some of your simpler cities, that there was so much bad work done. I found, where I went, bad wall-papers horribly designed, and coloured carpets, and that old offender the horse-hair sofa, whose stolid look of indifference is always so depressing. I found meaningless chandeliers and machine-made furniture, generally of rosewood, which creaked dismally under the weight of the ubiquitous interviewer. I came across the small iron stove which they always persist in decorating with machine-made ornaments, and which is as great a bore as a wet day or any other particularly dreadful institution. When unusual extravagance was indulged in, it was garnished with two funeral urns.

It must always be remembered that what is well and carefully made by an honest workman, after a rational design, increases in beauty and value as the years go on. The old furniture brought over by the Pilgrims, two hundred years ago, which I saw in New England, is just as good and as beautiful to-day as it was when it first came here. Now, what you must do is to bring artists and handicraftsmen together. Handicraftsmen cannot live, certainly cannot thrive, without such companionship. Separate these two and you rob art of all spiritual motive.

Having done this, you must place your workman in the midst of beautiful surroundings. The artist is not dependent on the visible and the tangible. He has his visions and his dreams to feed on. But the workman must see lovely forms as he goes to his work in the morning and returns at eventide. And, in connection with this, I want to assure you that noble and beautiful designs are never the result of idle fancy or purposeless day-dreaming. They come only as the accumulation of habits of long and delightful observation. And yet such things may not be taught. Right ideas concerning them can certainly be obtained only by those who have been accustomed to rooms that are beautiful and colours that are satisfying.

Perhaps one of the most difficult things for us to do is to choose a notable and joyous dress for men. There would be more joy in life if we were to accustom ourselves to use all the beautiful colours we can in fashioning our own clothes. The dress of the future, I think, will use drapery to a great extent and will abound with joyous colour. At present we have lost all nobility of dress and, in doing so, have almost annihilated the modern sculptor. And, in looking around at the figures which adorn our parks, one could almost wish that we had completely killed the noble art. To see the frock-coat of the drawing-room done in bronze, or the double waistcoat perpetuated in marble, adds a new horror to death. But indeed, in looking through the history of costume, seeking an answer to the questions we have propounded, there is little that is either beautiful or appropriate. One of the earliest forms is the Greek drapery which is exquisite for young girls. And then, I think we may be pardoned a little enthusiasm over the dress of the time of Charles I., so beautiful indeed, that in spite of its invention being with the Cavaliers it was copied by the Puritans. And the dress for the children of that time must not be passed over. It was a very golden age of the little ones. I do not think that they have ever looked so lovely as they do in the pictures of that time. The dress of the last century in England is also peculiarly gracious and graceful. There is nothing bizarre or strange about it, but it is full of harmony and beauty. In these days, when we have suffered dreadfully from the incursions of the modern milliner, we hear ladies boast that they do not wear a dress more than once. In the old days, when the dresses were decorated with beautiful designs and worked with exquisite embroidery, ladies rather took a pride in bringing out the garment and wearing it many times and handing it down to their daughters—a process that would, I think, be quite appreciated by a modern husband when called upon to settle his wife's bills.

And how shall men dress? Men say that they do not particularly care how they dress, and that it is little matter. I am bound to reply that I do not think that you do. In all my journeys through the country, the only well-dressed men that I saw—and in saying this I earnestly deprecate the polished indignation of your Fifth Avenue dandies—were the Western miners. Their wide-brimmed hats, which shaded their faces from the sun and protected them from the rain, and the cloak, which is by far the most beautiful piece of drapery ever invented, may well be dwelt on with admiration. Their high boots, too, were sensible and practical. They wore only what was comfortable, and therefore beautiful. As I looked at them I could not help thinking with regret of the time when these picturesque miners would have made their fortunes and would go East to assume again all the abominations of modern fashionable attire. Indeed, so concerned was I that I made some of them promise that when they again appeared in the more crowded scenes of Eastern civilisation they would still continue to wear their lovely costume. But I do not believe they will.

Now, what America wants to-day is a school of rational art. Bad art is a great deal worse than no art at all. You must show your workmen specimens of good work so that they come to know what is simple and true and beautiful. To that end I would have you have a museum attached to these schools—not one of those dreadful modern institutions where there is a stuffed and very dusty giraffe, and a case or two of fossils, but a place where there are gathered examples of art decoration from various periods and countries. Such a place is the South Kensington Museum in London, whereon we build greater hopes for the future than on any other one thing. There I go every Saturday night, when the museum is open later than usual, to see the handicraftsman, the wood-worker, the glass-blower and the worker in metals. And it is here that the man of refinement and culture comes face to face with the workman who ministers to his joy. He comes to know more of the nobility of the workman, and the workman, feeling the appreciation, comes to know more of the nobility of his work.

You have too many white walls. More colour is wanted. You should have such men as Whistler among you to teach you the beauty and joy of colour. Take Mr. Whistler's 'Symphony in White,' which you no doubt have imagined to be something quite bizarre. It is nothing of the sort. Think of a cool grey sky flecked here and there with white clouds, a grey ocean and three wonderfully beautiful figures robed in white, leaning over the water and dropping white flowers from their fingers. Here is no extensive intellectual scheme to trouble you, and no metaphysics of which we have had quite enough in art. But if the simple and unaided colour strike the right key-note, the whole conception is made clear. I regard Mr. Whistler's famous Peacock Room as the finest thing in colour and art decoration which the world has known since Correggio painted that wonderful room in Italy where the little children are dancing on the walls. Mr. Whistler finished another room just before I came away—a breakfast room in blue and yellow. The ceiling was a light blue, the cabinet-work and the furniture were of a yellow wood, the curtains at the windows were white and worked in yellow, and when the table was set for breakfast with dainty blue china nothing can be conceived at once so simple and so joyous.

The fault which I have observed in most of your rooms is that there is apparent no definite scheme of colour. Everything is not attuned to a key-note as it should be. The apartments are crowded with pretty things which have no relation to one another. Again, your artists must decorate what is more simply useful. In your art schools I found no attempt to decorate such things as the vessels for water. I know of nothing uglier than the ordinary jug or pitcher. A museum could be filled with the different kinds of water vessels which are used in hot countries. Yet we continue to submit to the depressing jug with the handle all on one side. I do not see the wisdom of decorating dinner-plates with sunsets and soup-plates with moonlight scenes. I do not think it adds anything to the pleasure of the canvas-back duck to take it out of such glories. Besides, we do not want a soup-plate whose bottom seems to vanish in the distance. One feels neither safe nor comfortable under such conditions. In fact, I did not find in the art schools of the country that the difference was explained between decorative and imaginative art.

The conditions of art should be simple. A great deal more depends upon the heart than upon the head. Appreciation of art is not secured by any elaborate scheme of learning. Art requires a good healthy atmosphere. The motives for art are still around about us as they were round about the ancients. And the subjects are also easily found by the earnest sculptor and the painter. Nothing is more picturesque and graceful than a man at work. The artist who goes to the children's playground, watches them at their sport and sees the boy stoop to tie his shoe, will find the same themes that engaged the attention of the ancient Greeks, and such observation and the illustrations which follow will do much to correct that foolish impression that mental and physical beauty are always divorced.

To you, more than perhaps to any other country, has Nature been generous in furnishing material for art workers to work in. You have marble quarries where the stone is more beautiful in colour than any the Greeks ever had for their beautiful work, and yet day after day I am confronted with the great building of some stupid man who has used the beautiful material as if it were not precious almost beyond speech. Marble should not be used save by noble workmen. There is nothing which gave me a greater sense of barrenness in travelling through the country than the entire absence of wood carving on your houses. Wood carving is the simplest of the decorative arts. In Switzerland the little barefooted boy beautifies the porch of his father's house with examples of skill in this direction. Why should not American boys do a great deal more and better than Swiss boys?

There is nothing to my mind more coarse in conception and more vulgar in execution than modern jewellery. This is something that can easily be corrected. Something better should be made out of the beautiful gold which is stored up in your mountain hollows and strewn along your river beds. When I was at Leadville and reflected that all the shining silver that I saw coming from the mines would be made into ugly dollars, it made me sad. It should be made into something more permanent. The golden gates at Florence are as beautiful to-day as when Michael Angelo saw them.

We should see more of the workman than we do. We should not be content to have the salesman stand between us—the salesman who knows nothing of what he is selling save that he is charging a great deal too much for it. And watching the workman will teach that most important lesson—the nobility of all rational workmanship.

I said in my last lecture that art would create a new brotherhood among men by furnishing a universal language. I said that under its beneficent influences war might pass away. Thinking this, what place can I ascribe to art in our education? If children grow up among all fair and lovely things, they will grow to love beauty and detest ugliness before they know the reason why. If you go into a house where everything is coarse, you find things chipped and broken and unsightly. Nobody exercises any care. If everything is dainty and delicate, gentleness and refinement of manner are unconsciously acquired. When I was in San Francisco I used to visit the Chinese Quarter frequently. There I used to watch a great hulking Chinese workman at his task of digging, and used to see him every day drink his tea from a little cup as delicate in texture as the petal of a flower, whereas in all the grand hotels of the land, where thousands of dollars have been lavished on great gilt mirrors and gaudy columns, I have been given my coffee or my chocolate in cups an inch and a quarter thick. I think I have deserved something nicer.

The art systems of the past have been devised by philosophers who looked upon human beings as obstructions. They have tried to educate boys' minds before they had any. How much better it would be in these early years to teach children to use their hands in the rational service of mankind. I would have a workshop attached to every school, and one hour a day given up to the teaching of simple decorative arts. It would be a golden hour to the children. And you would soon raise up a race of handicraftsmen who would transform the face of your country. I have seen only one such school in the United States, and this was in Philadelphia and was founded by my friend Mr. Leyland. I stopped there yesterday and have brought some of the work here this afternoon to show you. Here are two disks of beaten brass: the designs on them are beautiful, the workmanship is simple, and the entire result is satisfactory. The work was done by a little boy twelve years old. This is a wooden bowl decorated by a little girl of thirteen. The design is lovely and the colouring delicate and pretty. Here you see a piece of beautiful wood carving accomplished by a little boy of nine. In such work as this, children learn sincerity in art. They learn to abhor the liar in art—the man who paints wood to look like iron, or iron to look like stone. It is a practical school of morals. No better way is there to learn to love Nature than to understand Art. It dignifies every flower of the field. And, the boy who sees the thing of beauty which a bird on the wing becomes when transferred to wood or canvas will probably not throw the customary stone. What we want is something spiritual added to life. Nothing is so ignoble that Art cannot sanctify it.

ART AND THE HANDICRAFTSMAN

The fragments of which this lecture is composed are taken entirely from the original manuscripts which have but recently been discovered. It is not certain that they all belong to the same lecture, nor that all were written at the same period. Some portions were written in Philadelphia in 1882.

People often talk as if there was an opposition between what is beautiful and what is useful. There is no opposition to beauty except ugliness: all things are either beautiful or ugly, and utility will be always on the side of the beautiful thing, because beautiful decoration is always on the side of the beautiful thing, because beautiful decoration is always an expression of the use you put a thing to and the value placed on it. No workman will beautifully decorate bad work, nor can you possibly get good handicraftsmen or workmen without having beautiful designs. You should be quite sure of that. If you have poor and worthless designs in any craft or trade you will get poor and worthless workmen only, but the minute you have noble and beautiful designs, then you get men of power and intellect and feeling to work for you. By having good designs you have workmen who work not merely with their hands but with their hearts and heads too; otherwise you will get merely the fool or the loafer to work for you.

That the beauty of life is a thing of no moment, I suppose few people would venture to assert. And yet most civilised people act as if it were of none, and in so doing are wronging both themselves and those that are to come after them. For that beauty which is meant by art is no mere accident of human life which people can take or leave, but a positive necessity of life if we are to live as nature meant us to, that is to say unless we are content to be less than men.

Do not think that the commercial spirit which is the basis of your life and cities here is opposed to art. Who built the beautiful cities of the world but commercial men and commercial men only? Genoa built by its traders,

Florence by its bankers, and Venice, most lovely of all, by its noble and honest merchants.

I do not wish you, remember, 'to build a new Pisa,' nor to bring 'the life or the decorations of the thirteenth century back again.' 'The circumstances with which you must surround your workmen are those' of modern American life, 'because the designs you have now to ask for from your workmen are such as will make modern' American 'life beautiful.' The art we want is the art based on all the inventions of modern civilisation, and to suit all the needs of nineteenth-century life.

Do you think, for instance, that we object to machinery? I tell you we reverence it; we reverence it when it does its proper work, when it relieves man from ignoble and soulless labour, not when it seeks to do that which is valuable only when wrought by the hands and hearts of men. Let us have no machine-made ornament at all; it is all bad and worthless and ugly. And let us not mistake the means of civilisation for the end of civilisation; steam-engine, telephone and the like, are all wonderful, but remember that their value depends entirely on the noble uses we make of them, on the noble spirit in which we employ them, not on the things themselves.

It is, no doubt, a great advantage to talk to a man at the Antipodes through a telephone; its advantage depends entirely on the value of what the two men have to say to one another. If one merely shrieks slander through a tube and the other whispers folly into a wire, do not think that anybody is very much benefited by the invention.

The train that whirls an ordinary Englishman through Italy at the rate of forty miles an hour and finally sends him home without any memory of that lovely country but that he was cheated by a courier at Rome, or that he got a bad dinner at Verona, does not do him or civilisation much good. But that swift legion of fiery-footed engines that bore to the burning ruins of Chicago the loving help and generous treasure of the world was as noble and as beautiful as any golden troop of angels that ever fed the hungry and clothed the naked in the antique times. As beautiful, yes; all machinery may be beautiful when it is undecorated even. Do not seek to decorate it. We cannot but think all good machinery is graceful, also, the line of strength and the line of beauty being one.

Give then, as I said, to your workmen of to-day the bright and noble surroundings that you can yourself create. Stately and simple architecture for your cities, bright and simple dress for your men and women; those are the conditions of a real artistic movement. For the artist is not concerned primarily with any theory of life but with life itself, with the joy and loveliness that should come daily on eye and ear for a beautiful external world.

But the simplicity must not be barrenness nor the bright colour gaudy. For all beautiful colours are graduated colours, the colours that seem about to pass into one another's realm—colour without tone being like music without harmony, mere discord. Barren architecture, the vulgar and glaring advertisements that desecrate not merely your cities but every rock and river that I have seen yet in America—all this is not enough. A school of design we must have too in each city. It should be a stately and noble building, full of the best examples of the best art of the world. Furthermore, do not put your designers in a barren whitewashed room and bid them work in that depressing and colourless atmosphere as I have seen many of the American schools of design, but give them beautiful surroundings. Because you want to produce a permanent canon and standard of taste in your workman, he must have always by him and before him specimens of the best decorative art of the world, so that you can say to him: 'This is good work. Greek or Italian or Japanese wrought it so many years ago, but it is eternally young because eternally beautiful.' Work in this spirit and you will be sure to be right. Do not copy it, but work with the same love, the same reverence, the same freedom of imagination. You must teach him colour and design, how all beautiful colours are graduated colours and glaring colours the essence of vulgarity. Show him the quality of any beautiful work of nature like the rose, or any beautiful work of art like an Eastern carpet—being merely the exquisite gradation of colour, one tone answering another like the answering chords of a symphony. Teach him how the true designer is not he who makes the design and then colours it, but he who designs in colour, creates in colour, thinks in colour too. Show him how the most gorgeous stained-glass windows of Europe are filled with white glass, and the most gorgeous Eastern tapestry with toned colours—the primary colours in both places being set in the white glass, and the tone colours like brilliant jewels set in dusky gold. And then as regards design, show him how the real designer will take first any given limited space, little disk of silver, it may be, like a Greek coin, or wide expanse of fretted ceiling or lordly wall as Tintoret chose at Venice (it does not matter which), and to this limited space—the first condition of decoration being the limitation of the size of the material used—he will give the effect of its being filled with beautiful decoration, filled with it as a golden cup will be filled with wine, so complete that you should not be able to take away anything from it or add anything to it. For from a good piece of design you can take away nothing, nor can you add anything to it, each little bit of design being as absolutely necessary and as vitally important to the whole effect as a note or chord of music is for a sonata of Beethoven.

But I said the effect of its being so filled, because this, again, is of the essence of good design. With a simple spray of leaves and a bird in flight a Japanese artist will give you the impression that he has completely covered with lovely design the reed fan or lacquer cabinet at which he is working, merely because he knows the exact spot in which to place them. All good design depends on the texture of the utensil used and the use you wish to put it to. One of the first things I saw in an American school of design was a young lady painting a romantic moonlight landscape on a large round dish, and another young lady covering a set of dinner plates with a series of sunsets of the most remarkable colours. Let your ladies paint moonlight landscapes and sunsets, but do not let them paint them on dinner plates or dishes. Let them take canvas or paper for such work, but not clay or china. They are merely painting the wrong subjects on the wrong material, that is all. They have not been taught that every material and texture has certain qualities of its own. The design suitable for one is quite wrong for the other, just as the design which you should work on a flat table-cover ought to be quite different from the design you would work on a curtain, for the one will always be straight, the other broken into folds; and the use too one puts the object to should guide one in the choice of design. One does not want to eat one's terrapins off a romantic moonlight nor one's clams off a harrowing sunset.

Glory of sun and moon, let them be wrought for us by our landscape artist and be on the walls of the rooms we sit in to remind us of the undying beauty of the sunsets that fade and die, but do not let us eat our soup off them and send them down to the kitchen twice a day to be washed and scrubbed by the handmaid.

All these things are simple enough, yet nearly always forgotten. Your school of design here will teach your girls and your boys, your handicraftsmen of the future (for all your schools of art should be local schools, the schools of particular cities). We talk of the Italian school of painting, but there is no Italian school; there were the schools of each city. Every town in Italy, from Venice itself, queen of the sea, to the little hill fortress of Perugia, each had its own school of art, each different and all beautiful.

So do not mind what art Philadelphia or New York is having, but make by the hands of your own citizens beautiful art for the joy of your own citizens, for you have here the primary elements of a great artistic movement.

For, believe me, the conditions of art are much simpler than people imagine. For the noblest art one requires a clear healthy atmosphere, not polluted as the air of our English cities is by the smoke and grime and horridness which comes from open furnace and from factory chimney. You must have strong, sane, healthy physique among your men and women. Sickly or idle or melancholy people do not do much in art. And lastly, you require a sense of individualism about each man and woman, for this is the essence of art—a desire on the part of man to express himself in the noblest way possible. And this is the reason that the grandest art of the world always came from a republic: Athens, Venice, and Florence—there were no kings there and so their art was as noble and simple as sincere. But if you want to know what kind of art the folly of kings will impose on a country look at the decorative art of France under the grand monarque, under Louis the Fourteenth; the gaudy gilt furniture writhing under a sense of its own horror and ugliness, with a nymph smirking at every angle and a dragon mouthing on every claw. Unreal and monstrous art this, and fit only for such periwigged pomposities as the nobility of France at that time, but not at all fit for you or me. We do not want the rich to possess more beautiful things but the poor to create more beautiful things; for ever man is poor who cannot create. Nor shall the art which you and I need be merely a purple robe woven by a slave and thrown over the whitened body of some leprous king to adorn or to conceal the sin of his luxury, but rather shall it be the noble and beautiful expression of a people's noble and beautiful life. Art shall be again the most glorious of all the chords through which the spirit of a great nation finds its noblest utterance.

All around you, I said, lie the conditions for a great artistic movement for every great art. Let us think of one of them; a sculptor, for instance.

If a modern sculptor were to come and say, 'Very well, but where can one find subjects for sculpture out of men who wear frock-coats and chimney-pot hats?' I would tell him to go to the docks of a great city and watch the men loading or unloading the stately ships, working at wheel or windlass, hauling at rope or gangway. I have never watched a man do anything useful who has not been graceful at some moment of his labour: it is only the loafer and the idle saunterer who is as useless and uninteresting to the artist as he is to himself. I would ask the sculptor to go with me to any of your schools or universities, to the running ground and gymnasium, to watch the young men start for a race, hurling quoit or club, kneeling to tie their shoes before leaping, stepping from the boat or bending to the oar, and to carve them; and when he was weary of cities I would ask him to come to your fields and meadows to watch the reaper with his sickle and the cattle-driver with lifted lasso. For if a man cannot find the noblest motives for his art in such simple daily things as a woman drawing water from the well or a man leaning with his scythe, he will not find them anywhere at all. Gods and goddesses the Greek carved because he loved them; saint and king the Goth because he believed in them. But you, you do not care much for Greek gods and goddesses, and you are perfectly and entirely right; and you do not think much of kings either, and you are quite right. But what you do love are your own men and women, your own flowers and fields, your own hills and mountains, and these are what your art should represent to you.

Ours has been the first movement which has brought the handicraftsman and the artist together, for remember that by separating the one from the other you do ruin to both; you rob the one of all spiritual motive and all imaginative joy, you isolate the other from all real technical perfection. The two greatest schools of art in the world, the sculptor at Athens and the school of painting at Venice, had their origin entirely in a long succession of simple and earnest handicraftsmen. It was the Greek potter who taught the sculptor that restraining influence of design which was the glory of the Parthenon; it was the Italian decorator of chests and household goods who kept Venetian painting always true to its primary pictorial condition of noble colour. For we should remember that all the arts are fine arts and all the arts decorative arts. The greatest triumph of Italian painting was the decoration of a pope's chapel in Rome and the wall of a room in Venice. Michael Angelo wrought the one, and Tintoret, the dyer's son, the other. And the little 'Dutch landscape, which you put over your sideboard to-day, and between the windows to-morrow, is' no less a glorious 'piece of work than the extents of field and forest with which Benozzo has made green and beautiful the once melancholy arcade of the Campo Santo at Pisa,' as Ruskin says.

Do not imitate the works of a nation, Greek or Japanese, Italian or English; but their artistic spirit of design and their artistic attitude to-day, their own world, you should absorb but imitate never, copy never. Unless you can make as beautiful a design in painted china or embroidered screen or beaten brass out of your American turkey as the Japanese does out of his grey silver-winged stork, you will never do anything. Let the Greek carve his lions and the Goth his dragons: buffalo and wild deer are the animals for you.

Golden rod and aster and rose and all the flowers that cover your valleys in the spring and your hills in the autumn: let them be the flowers for your art. Not merely has Nature given you the noblest motives for a new school of decoration, but to you above all other countries has she given the utensils to work in.

You have quarries of marble richer than Pentelicus, more varied than Paros, but do not build a great white square house of marble and think that it is beautiful, or that you are using marble nobly. If you build in marble you must either carve it into joyous decoration, like the lives of dancing children that adorn the marble castles of the Loire, or fill it with beautiful sculpture,

110

frieze and pediment, as the Greeks did, or inlay it with other coloured marbles as they did in Venice. Otherwise you had better build in simple red brick as your Puritan fathers, with no pretence and with some beauty. Do not treat your marble as if it was ordinary stone and build a house of mere blocks of it. For it is indeed a precious stone, this marble of yours, and only workmen of nobility of invention and delicacy of hand should be allowed to touch it at all, carving it into noble statues or into beautiful decoration, or inlaying it with other coloured marbles: for 'the true colours of architecture are those of natural stone, and I would fain see them taken advantage of to the full. Every variety is here, from pale yellow to purple passing through orange, red, and brown, entirely at your command; nearly every kind of green and grey also is attainable, and with these and with pure white what harmony might you not achieve. Of stained and variegated stone the quantity is unlimited, the kinds innumerable. Were brighter colours required, let glass, and gold protected by glass, be used in mosaic, a kind of work as durable as the solid stone and incapable of losing its lustre by time. And let the painter's work be reserved for the shadowed loggia and inner chamber.

'This is the true and faithful way of building. Where this cannot be, the device of external colouring may indeed be employed without dishonour— but it must be with the warning reflection that a time will come when such aids will pass away and when the building will be judged in its lifelessness, dying the death of the dolphin. Better the less bright, more enduring fabric. The transparent alabasters of San Miniato and the mosaics of Saint Mark's are more warmly filled and more brightly touched by every return of morning and evening, while the hues of the Gothic cathedrals have died like the iris out of the cloud, and the temples, whose azure and purple once flamed above the Grecian promontory, stand in their faded whiteness like snows which the sunset has left cold.'—Ruskin, Seven Lamps of Architecture, II.

I do not know anything so perfectly commonplace in design as most modern jewellery. How easy for you to change that and to produce goldsmiths' work that would be a joy to all of us. The gold is ready for you in unexhausted treasure, stored up in the mountain hollow or strewn on the river sand, and was not given to you merely for barren speculation. There should be some better record of it left in your history than the merchant's panic and the ruined home. We do not remember often enough how constantly the history of a great nation will live in and by its art. Only a few thin wreaths of beaten gold remain to tell us of the stately empire of Etruria; and, while from the streets of Florence the noble knight and haughty duke have long since passed away, the gates which the simple goldsmith Ghiberti made for their pleasure still guard their lovely house of baptism, worthy still of the praise of Michael Angelo who called them worthy to be the Gates of Paradise.

Have then your school of design, search out your workmen and, when you find one who has delicacy of hand and that wonder of invention necessary for goldsmiths' work, do not leave him to toil in obscurity and dishonour and have a great glaring shop and two great glaring shop-boys in it (not to take your orders: they never do that; but to force you to buy something you do not want at all). When you want a thing wrought in gold, goblet or shield for the feast, necklace or wreath for the women, tell him what you like most in decoration, flower or wreath, bird in flight or hound in the chase, image of the woman you love or the friend you honour. Watch him as he beats out the gold into those thin plates delicate as the petals of a yellow rose, or draws it into the long wires like tangled sunbeams at dawn. Whoever that workman be, help him, cherish him, and you will have such lovely work from his hand as will be a joy to you for all time.

This is the spirit of our movement in England, and this is the spirit in which we would wish you to work, making eternal by your art all that is noble in your men and women, stately in your lakes and mountains, beautiful in your own flowers and natural life. We want to see that you have nothing in your houses that has not been a joy to the man who made it, and is not a joy to those that use it. We want to see you create an art made by the hands of the people to please the hearts of the people too. Do you like this spirit or not? Do you think it simple and strong, noble in its aim, and beautiful in its result? I know you do.

Folly and slander have their own way for a little time, but for a little time only. You now know what we mean: you will be able to estimate what is said of us—its value and its motive.

112

There should be a law that no ordinary newspaper should be allowed to write about art. The harm they do by their foolish and random writing it would be impossible to overestimate—not to the artist but to the public, blinding them to all, but harming the artist not at all. Without them we would judge a man simply by his work; but at present the newspapers are trying hard to induce the public to judge a sculptor, for instance, never by his statues but by the way he treats his wife; a painter by the amount of his income and a poet by the colour of his neck-tie. I said there should be a law, but there is really no necessity for a new law: nothing could be easier than to bring the ordinary critic under the head of the criminal classes. But let us leave such an inartistic subject and return to beautiful and comely things, remembering that the art which would represent the spirit of modern newspapers would be exactly the art which you and I want to avoid—grotesque art, malice mocking you from every gateway, slander sneering at you from every corner.

Perhaps you may be surprised at my talking of labour and the workman. You have heard of me, I fear, through the medium of your somewhat imaginative newspapers as, if not a 'Japanese young man,' at least a young man to whom the rush and clamour and reality of the modern world were distasteful, and whose greatest difficulty in life was the difficulty of living up to the level of his blue china—a paradox from which England has not yet recovered.

Well, let me tell you how it first came to me at all to create an artistic movement in England, a movement to show the rich what beautiful things they might enjoy and the poor what beautiful things they might create.

One summer afternoon in Oxford—'that sweet city with her dreaming spires,' lovely as Venice in its splendour, noble in its learning as Rome, down the long High Street that winds from tower to tower, past silent cloister and stately gateway, till it reaches that long, grey seven-arched bridge which Saint Mary used to guard (used to, I say, because they are now pulling it down to build a tramway and a light cast-iron bridge in its place, desecrating the loveliest city in England)—well, we were coming down the street—a troop of young men, some of them like myself only nineteen, going to river or tennis-court or cricket-field—when Ruskin going up to lecture in cap and gown met us. He seemed troubled and prayed us to go back with him to his lecture, which a few of us did, and there he spoke to us not on art this time but on life, saying that it seemed to him to be wrong that all the best physique and strength of the young men in England should be spent aimlessly on cricket ground or river, without any result at all except that if one rowed well one got a pewter-pot, and if one made a good score, a cane-handled bat. He thought, he said, that we should be working at something that would do good to other people, at something by which we might show that in all labour there was something noble. Well, we were a good deal moved, and said we would do anything he wished. So he went out round Oxford and found two villages, Upper and Lower Hinksey, and between them there lay a great swamp, so that the villagers could not pass from one to the other without many miles of a round. And when we came back in winter he asked us to help him to make a road across this morass for these village people to use. So out we went, day after day, and learned how to lay levels and to break stones, and to wheel barrows along a plank—a very difficult thing to do. And Ruskin worked with us in the mist and rain and mud of an Oxford winter, and our friends and our enemies came out and mocked us from the bank. We did not mind it much then, and we did not mind it afterwards at all, but worked away for two months at our road. And what became of the road? Well, like a bad lecture it ended abruptly—in the middle of the swamp. Ruskin going away to Venice, when we came back for the next term there was no leader, and the 'diggers,' as they called us, fell asunder. And I felt that if there was enough spirit amongst the young men to go out to such work as road-making for the sake of a noble ideal of life, I could from them create an artistic movement that might change, as it has changed, the face of England. So I sought them out—leader they would call me—but there was no leader: we were all searchers only and we were bound to each other by noble friendship and by noble art. There was none of us idle: poets most of us, so ambitious were we: painters some of us, or workers in metal or modellers, determined that we would try and create for ourselves beautiful work: for the handicraftsman beautiful work, for those who love us poems and pictures, for those who love us not epigrams and paradoxes and scorn.

Well, we have done something in England and we will do something more. Now, I do not want you, believe me, to ask your brilliant young men, your beautiful young girls, to go out and make a road on a swamp for any village in America, but I think you might each of you have some art to practise.

We must have, as Emerson said, a mechanical craft for our culture, a basis for our higher accomplishments in the work of our hands—the uselessness of most people's hands seems to me one of the most unpractical things. 'No separation from labour can be without some loss of power or truth to the seer,' says Emerson again. The heroism which would make on us the impression of Epaminondas must be that of a domestic conqueror. The hero of the future is he who shall bravely and gracefully subdue this Gorgon of fashion and of convention.

When you have chosen your own part, abide by it, and do not weakly try and reconcile yourself with the world. The heroic cannot be the common nor the common the heroic. Congratulate yourself if you have done something strange and extravagant and broken the monotony of a decorous age.

And lastly, let us remember that art is the one thing which Death cannot harm. The little house at Concord may be desolate, but the wisdom of New England's Plato is not silenced nor the brilliancy of that Attic genius dimmed: the lips of Longfellow are still musical for us though his dust be turning into the flowers which he loved: and as it is with the greater artists, poet and philosopher and song-bird, so let it be with you.

LECTURE TO ART STUDENTS

Delivered to the Art students of the Royal Academy at their Club in Golden Square, Westminster, on June 30, 1883. The text is taken from the original manuscript.

In the lecture which it is my privilege to deliver before you to-night I do not desire to give you any abstract definition of beauty at all. For we who are working in art cannot accept any theory of beauty in exchange for beauty itself, and, so far from desiring to isolate it in a formula appealing to the intellect, we, on the contrary, seek to materialise it in a form that gives joy to the soul through the senses. We want to create it, not to define it. The definition should follow the work: the work should not adapt itself to the definition.

Nothing, indeed, is more dangerous to the young artist than any conception of ideal beauty: he is constantly led by it either into weak prettiness or lifeless abstraction: whereas to touch the ideal at all you must not strip it of vitality. You must find it in life and re-create it in art.

While, then, on the one hand I do not desire to give you any philosophy of beauty—for, what I want to-night is to investigate how we can create art, not how we can talk of it—on the other hand, I do not wish to deal with anything like a history of English art.

To begin with, such an expression as English art is a meaningless expression. One might just as well talk of English mathematics. Art is the science of beauty, and Mathematics the science of truth: there is no national school of either. Indeed, a national school is a provincial school, merely. Nor is there any such thing as a school of art even. There are merely artists, that is all.

And as regards histories of art, they are quite valueless to you unless you are seeking the ostentatious oblivion of an art professorship. It is of no use to you to know the date of Perugino or the birthplace of Salvator Rosa: all that you should learn about art is to know a good picture when you see it, and a bad picture when you see it. As regards the date of the artist, all good work looks perfectly modern: a piece of Greek sculpture, a portrait of Velasquez— they are always modern, always of our time. And as regards the nationality of the artist, art is not national but universal. As regards archæology, then, avoid it altogether: archæology is merely the science of making excuses for bad art; it is the rock on which many a young artist founders and shipwrecks; it is the abyss from which no artist, old or young, ever returns. Or, if he does return, he is so covered with the dust of ages and the mildew of time, that he is quite unrecognisable as an artist, and has to conceal himself for the rest of his days under the cap of a professor, or as a mere illustrator of ancient history. How worthless archæology is in art you can estimate by the fact of its being so popular. Popularity is the crown of laurel which the world puts on bad art. Whatever is popular is wrong.

As I am not going to talk to you, then, about the philosophy of the beautiful, or the history of art, you will ask me what I am going to talk about. The subject of my lecture to-night is what makes an artist and what does the artist make; what are the relations of the artist to his surroundings, what is the education the artist should get, and what is the quality of a good work of art.

Now, as regards the relations of the artist to his surroundings, by which I mean the age and country in which he is born. All good art, as I said before, has nothing to do with any particular century; but this universality is the quality of the work of art; the conditions that produce that quality are different. And what, I think, you should do is to realise completely your age in order completely to abstract yourself from it; remembering that if you are an artist at all, you will be not the mouthpiece of a century, but the master of eternity, that all art rests on a principle, and that mere temporal considerations are no principle at all; and that those who advise you to make your art representative of the nineteenth century are advising you to produce an art which your children, when you have them, will think old-fashioned. But you will tell me this is an inartistic age, and we are an inartistic people, and the artist suffers much in this nineteenth century of ours.

Of course he does. I, of all men, am not going to deny that. But

117

remember that there never has been an artistic age, or an artistic people, since the beginning of the world. The artist has always been, and will always be, an exquisite exception. There is no golden age of art; only artists who have produced what is more golden than gold.

What, you will say to me, the Greeks? were not they an artistic people?

Well, the Greeks certainly not, but, perhaps, you mean the Athenians, the citizens of one out of a thousand cities.

Do you think that they were an artistic people? Take them even at the time of their highest artistic development, the latter part of the fifth century before Christ, when they had the greatest poets and the greatest artists of the antique world, when the Parthenon rose in loveliness at the bidding of a Phidias, and the philosopher spake of wisdom in the shadow of the painted portico, and tragedy swept in the perfection of pageant and pathos across the marble of the stage. Were they an artistic people then? Not a bit of it. What is an artistic people but a people who love their artists and understand their art? The Athenians could do neither.

How did they treat Phidias? To Phidias we owe the great era, not merely in Greek, but in all art—I mean of the introduction of the use of the living model.

And what would you say if all the English bishops, backed by the English people, came down from Exeter Hall to the Royal Academy one day and took off Sir Frederick Leighton in a prison van to Newgate on the charge of having allowed you to make use of the living model in your designs for sacred pictures?

Would you not cry out against the barbarism and the Puritanism of such an idea? Would you not explain to them that the worst way to honour God is to dishonour man who is made in His image, and is the work of His hands; and, that if one wants to paint Christ one must take the most Christlike person one can find, and if one wants to paint the Madonna, the purest girl one knows?

Would you not rush off and burn down Newgate, if necessary, and say

118

that such a thing was without parallel in history?

Without parallel? Well, that is exactly what the Athenians did.

In the room of the Parthenon marbles, in the British Museum, you will see a marble shield on the wall. On it there are two figures; one of a man whose face is half hidden, the other of a man with the godlike lineaments of Pericles. For having done this, for having introduced into a bas relief, taken from Greek sacred history, the image of the great statesman who was ruling Athens at the time, Phidias was flung into prison and there, in the common gaol of Athens, died, the supreme artist of the old world.

And do you think that this was an exceptional case? The sign of a Philistine age is the cry of immorality against art, and this cry was raised by the Athenian people against every great poet and thinker of their day—Æschylus, Euripides, Socrates. It was the same with Florence in the thirteenth century. Good handicrafts are due to guilds, not to the people. The moment the guilds lost their power and the people rushed in, beauty and honesty of work died.

And so, never talk of an artistic people; there never has been such a thing.

But, perhaps, you will tell me that the external beauty of the world has almost entirely passed away from us, that the artist dwells no longer in the midst of the lovely surroundings which, in ages past, were the natural inheritance of every one, and that art is very difficult in this unlovely town of ours, where, as you go to your work in the morning, or return from it at eventide, you have to pass through street after street of the most foolish and stupid architecture that the world has ever seen; architecture, where every lovely Greek form is desecrated and defiled, and every lovely Gothic form defiled and desecrated, reducing three-fourths of the London houses to being, merely, like square boxes of the vilest proportions, as gaunt as they are grimy, and as poor as they are pretentious—the hall door always of the wrong colour, and the windows of the wrong size, and where, even when wearied of the houses you turn to contemplate the street itself, you have nothing to look at but chimney-pot hats, men with sandwich boards, vermilion letter-boxes, and do that even at the risk of being run over by an emerald-green omnibus.

Is not art difficult, you will say to me, in such surroundings as these? Of course it is difficult, but then art was never easy; you yourselves would not wish it to be easy; and, besides, nothing is worth doing except what the world says is impossible.

Still, you do not care to be answered merely by a paradox. What are the relations of the artist to the external world, and what is the result of the loss of beautiful surroundings to you, is one of the most important questions of modern art; and there is no point on which Mr. Ruskin so insists as that the decadence of art has come from the decadence of beautiful things; and that when the artist cannot feed his eye on beauty, beauty goes from his work.

I remember in one of his lectures, after describing the sordid aspect of a great English city, he draws for us a picture of what were the artistic surroundings long ago.

Think, he says, in words of perfect and picturesque imagery, whose beauty I can but feebly echo, think of what was the scene which presented itself, in his afternoon walk, to a designer of the Gothic school of Pisa—Nino Pisano or any of his men: [206]

> On each side of a bright river he saw rise a line of brighter palaces, arched and pillared, and inlaid with deep red porphyry, and with serpentine; along the quays before their gates were riding troops of knights, noble in face and form, dazzling in crest and shield; horse and man one labyrinth of quaint colour and gleaming light—the purple, and silver, and scarlet fringes flowing over the strong limbs and clashing mall, like sea-waves over rocks at sunset. Opening on each side from the river were gardens, courts, and cloisters; long successions of white pillars among wreaths of vine; leaping of fountains through buds of pomegranate and orange: and still along the garden-paths, and under and through the crimson of the pomegranate shadows, moving slowly, groups of the fairest women that Italy ever saw—fairest, because purest and thoughtfullest; trained in all high knowledge, as in all courteous art—in dance, in song, in sweet wit, in lofty learning, in

loftier courage, in loftiest love—able alike to cheer, to enchant, or save, the souls of men. Above all this scenery of perfect human life, rose dome and bell-tower, burning with white alabaster and gold: beyond dome and bell-tower the slopes of mighty hills hoary with olive; far in the north, above a purple sea of peaks of solemn Apennine, the clear, sharp-cloven Carrara mountains sent up their steadfast flames of marble summit into amber sky; the great sea itself, scorching with expanse of light, stretching from their feet to the Gorgonian isles; and over all these, ever present, near or far—seen through the leaves of vine, or imaged with all its march of clouds in the Arno's stream, or set with its depth of blue close against the golden hair and burning cheek of lady and knight,—that untroubled and sacred sky, which was to all men, in those days of innocent faith, indeed the unquestioned abode of spirits, as the earth was of men; and which opened straight through its gates of cloud and veils of dew into the awfulness of the eternal world;—a heaven in which every cloud that passed was literally the chariot of an angel, and every ray of its Evening and Morning streamed from the throne of God.

What think you of that for a school of design?

And then look at the depressing, monotonous appearance of any modern city, the sombre dress of men and women, the meaningless and barren architecture, the colourless and dreadful surroundings. Without a beautiful national life, not sculpture merely, but all the arts will die.

Well, as regards the religious feeling of the close of the passage, I do not think I need speak about that. Religion springs from religious feeling, art from artistic feeling: you never get one from the other; unless you have the right root you will not get the right flower; and, if a man sees in a cloud the chariot of an angel, he will probably paint it very unlike a cloud.

But, as regards the general idea of the early part of that lovely bit of prose, is it really true that beautiful surroundings are necessary for the artist? I think not; I am sure not. Indeed, to me the most inartistic thing in this age of ours is not the indifference of the public to beautiful things, but the indifference of the artist to the things that are called ugly. For, to the real artist, nothing is beautiful or ugly in itself at all. With the facts of the object he has nothing to do, but with its appearance only, and appearance is a matter of light and shade, of masses, of position, and of value.

Appearance is, in fact, a matter of effect merely, and it is with the effects of nature that you have to deal, not with the real condition of the object. What you, as painters, have to paint is not things as they are but things as they seem to be, not things as they are but things as they are not.

No object is so ugly that, under certain conditions of light and shade, or proximity to other things, it will not look beautiful; no object is so beautiful that, under certain conditions, it will not look ugly. I believe that in every twenty-four hours what is beautiful looks ugly, and what is ugly looks beautiful, once.

And, the commonplace character of so much of our English painting seems to me due to the fact that so many of our young artists look merely at what we may call 'ready-made beauty,' whereas you exist as artists not to copy beauty but to create it in your art, to wait and watch for it in nature.

What would you say of a dramatist who would take nobody but virtuous people as characters in his play? Would you not say he was missing half of life? Well, of the young artist who paints nothing but beautiful things, I say he misses one half of the world.

Do not wait for life to be picturesque, but try and see life under picturesque conditions. These conditions you can create for yourself in your studio, for they are merely conditions of light. In nature, you must wait for them, watch for them, choose them; and, if you wait and watch, come they will.

In Gower Street at night you may see a letter-box that is picturesque: on the Thames Embankment you may see picturesque policemen. Even Venice is not always beautiful, nor France.

To paint what you see is a good rule in art, but to see what is worth painting is better. See life under pictorial conditions. It is better to live in a city of changeable weather than in a city of lovely surroundings.

Now, having seen what makes the artist, and what the artist makes, who is the artist? There is a man living amongst us who unites in himself all the qualities of the noblest art, whose work is a joy for all time, who is, himself, a master of all time. That man is Mr. Whistler.

* * * * *

But, you will say, modern dress, that is bad. If you cannot paint black cloth you could not have painted silken doublet. Ugly dress is better for art—facts of vision, not of the object.

What is a picture? Primarily, a picture is a beautifully coloured surface, merely, with no more spiritual message or meaning for you than an exquisite fragment of Venetian glass or a blue tile from the wall of Damascus. It is, primarily, a purely decorative thing, a delight to look at.

All archæological pictures that make you say 'How curious!' all sentimental pictures that make you say, 'How sad!' all historical pictures that make you say 'How interesting!' all pictures that do not immediately give you such artistic joy as to make you say 'How beautiful!' are bad pictures.

* * * * *

We never know what an artist is going to do. Of course not. The artist is not a specialist. All such divisions as animal painters, landscape painters, painters of Scotch cattle in an English mist, painters of English cattle in a Scotch mist, racehorse painters, bull-terrier painters, all are shallow. If a man is an artist he can paint everything.

The object of art is to stir the most divine and remote of the chords which make music in our soul; and colour is indeed, of itself a mystical presence on things, and tone a kind of sentinel.

Am I pleading, then, for mere technique? No. As long as there are any signs of technique at all, the picture is unfinished. What is finish? A picture is finished when all traces of work, and of the means employed to bring about the result, have disappeared.

In the case of handicraftsmen—the weaver, the potter, the smith—on their work are the traces of their hand. But it is not so with the painter; it is not so with the artist.

Art should have no sentiment about it but its beauty, no technique except what you cannot observe. One should be able to say of a picture not that it is 'well painted,' but that it is 'not painted.'

What is the difference between absolutely decorative art and a painting? Decorative art emphasises its material: imaginative art annihilates it. Tapestry shows its threads as part of its beauty: a picture annihilates its canvas: it shows nothing of it. Porcelain emphasises its glaze: water-colours reject the paper.

A picture has no meaning but its beauty, no message but its joy. That is the first truth about art that you must never lose sight of. A picture is a purely decorative thing.

LONDON MODELS

English Illustrated Magazine, January 1889.

Professional models are a purely modern invention. To the Greeks, for instance, they were quite unknown. Mr. Mahaffy, it is true, tells us that Pericles used to present peacocks to the great ladies of Athenian society in order to induce them to sit to his friend Phidias, and we know that Polygnotus introduced into his picture of the Trojan women the face of Elpinice, the celebrated sister of the great Conservative leader of the day, but these grandes dames clearly do not come under our category. As for the old masters, they undoubtedly made constant studies from their pupils and apprentices, and even their religious pictures are full of the portraits of their friends and relations, but they do not seem to have had the inestimable advantage of the existence of a class of people whose sole profession is to pose. In fact the model, in our sense of the word, is the direct creation of Academic Schools.

Every country now has its own models, except America. In New York, and even in Boston, a good model is so great a rarity that most of the artists are reduced to painting Niagara and millionaires. In Europe, however, it is different. Here we have plenty of models, and of every nationality. The Italian models are the best. The natural grace of their attitudes, as well as the wonderful picturesqueness of their colouring, makes them facile—often too facile—subjects for the painter's brush. The French models, though not so beautiful as the Italian, possess a quickness of intellectual sympathy, a capacity, in fact, of understanding the artist, which is quite remarkable. They have also a great command over the varieties of facial expression, are peculiarly dramatic, and can chatter the argot of the atelier as cleverly as the critic of the Gil Blas. The English models form a class entirely by themselves. They are not so picturesque as the Italian, nor so clever as the French, and they have absolutely no tradition, so to speak, of their order. Now and then some old veteran knocks at the studio door, and proposes to sit as Ajax defying the lightning, or as King Lear upon the blasted heath. One of them some time ago called on a popular painter who, happening at the moment to require his services, engaged him, and told him to begin by kneeling down in the attitude of prayer. 'Shall I be Biblical or Shakespearean, sir?' asked the veteran. 'Well—Shakespearean,' answered the artist, wondering by what subtle nuance of expression the model would convey the difference. 'All right, sir,' said the professor of posing, and he solemnly knelt down and began to wink with his left eye! This class, however, is dying out. As a rule the model, nowadays, is a pretty girl, from about twelve to twenty-five years of age, who knows nothing about art, cares less, and is merely anxious to earn seven or eight shillings a day without much trouble. English models rarely look at a picture, and never venture on any æsthetic theories. In fact, they realise very completely Mr. Whistler's idea of the function of an art critic, for they pass no criticisms at all. They accept all schools of art with the grand catholicity of the auctioneer, and sit to a fantastic young impressionist as readily as to a learned and laborious academician. They are neither for the Whistlerites nor against them; the quarrel between the school of facts and the school of effects touches them not; idealistic and naturalistic are words that convey no meaning to their ears; they merely desire that the studio shall be warm, and the lunch hot, for all charming artists give their models lunch.

As to what they are asked to do they are equally indifferent. On Monday they will don the rags of a beggar-girl for Mr. Pumper, whose pathetic pictures of modern life draw such tears from the public, and on Tuesday they will pose in a peplum for Mr. Phoebus, who thinks that all really artistic subjects are necessarily B.C. They career gaily through all centuries and through all costumes, and, like actors, are interesting only when they are not themselves. They are extremely good-natured, and very accommodating. 'What do you sit for?' said a young artist to a model who had sent him in her card (all models, by the way, have cards and a small black bag). 'Oh, for anything you like, sir,' said the girl, 'landscape if necessary!'

Intellectually, it must be acknowledged, they are Philistines, but physically they are perfect—at least some are. Though none of them can talk Greek, many can look Greek, which to a nineteenth-century painter is naturally of great importance. If they are allowed, they chatter a great deal, but they never say anything. Their observations are the only banalités heard in Bohemia. However, though they cannot appreciate the artist as artist, they are quite ready to appreciate the artist as a man. They are very sensitive to kindness, respect and generosity. A beautiful model who had sat for two years to one of our most distinguished English painters, got engaged to a street vendor of penny ices.

On her marriage the painter sent her a pretty wedding present, and received in return a nice letter of thanks with the following remarkable postscript: 'Never eat the green ices!'

When they are tired a wise artist gives them a rest. Then they sit in a chair and read penny dreadfuls, till they are roused from the tragedy of literature to take their place again in the tragedy of art. A few of them smoke cigarettes. This, however, is regarded by the other models as showing a want of seriousness, and is not generally approved of. They are engaged by the day and by the half-day. The tariff is a shilling an hour, to which great artists usually add an omnibus fare. The two best things about them are their extraordinary prettiness, and their extreme respectability. As a class they are very well behaved, particularly those who sit for the figure, a fact which is curious or natural according to the view one takes of human nature. They usually marry well, and sometimes they marry the artist. For an artist to marry his model is as fatal as for a gourmet to marry his cook: the one gets no sittings, and the other gets no dinners.

On the whole the English female models are very naïve, very natural, and very good-humoured. The virtues which the artist values most in them are prettiness and punctuality. Every sensible model consequently keeps a diary of her engagements, and dresses neatly. The bad season is, of course, the summer, when the artists are out of town. However, of late years some artists have engaged their models to follow them, and the wife of one of our most charming painters has often had three or four models under her charge in the country, so that the work of her husband and his friends should not be interrupted. In France the models migrate en masse to the little seaport villages or forest hamlets where the painters congregate. The English models, however, wait patiently in London, as a rule, till the artists come back. Nearly all of them live with their parents, and help to support the house. They have every qualification for being immortalised in art except that of beautiful hands. The hands of the English model are nearly always coarse and red.

As for the male models, there is the veteran whom we have mentioned above. He has all the traditions of the grand style, and is rapidly disappearing with the school he represents. An old man who talks about Fuseli is, of course, unendurable, and, besides, patriarchs have ceased to be fashionable subjects. Then there is the true Academy model. He is usually a man of thirty, rarely good-looking, but a perfect miracle of muscles. In fact he is the apotheosis of anatomy, and is so conscious of his own splendour that he tells you of his tibia and his thorax, as if no one else had anything of the kind. Then come the Oriental models. The supply of these is limited, but there are always about a dozen in London. They are very much sought after as they can remain immobile for hours, and generally possess lovely costumes. However, they have a very poor opinion of English art, which they regard as something between a vulgar personality and a commonplace photograph. Next we have the Italian youth who has come over specially to be a model, or takes to it when his organ is out of repair. He is often quite charming with his large melancholy eyes, his crisp hair, and his slim brown figure. It is true he eats garlic, but then he can stand like a faun and couch like a leopard, so he is forgiven. He is always full of pretty compliments, and has been known to have kind words of encouragement for even our greatest artists. As for the English lad of the same age, he never sits at all. Apparently he does not regard the career of a model as a serious profession. In any case he is rarely, if ever, to be got hold of. English boys, too, are difficult to find. Sometimes an ex-model who has a son will curl his hair, and wash his face, and bring him the round of the studios, all soap and shininess. The young school don't like him, but the older school do, and when he appears on the walls of the Royal Academy he is called The Infant Samuel. Occasionally also an artist catches a couple of gamins in the gutter and asks them to come to his studio. The first time they always appear, but after that they don't keep their appointments. They dislike sitting still, and have a strong and perhaps natural objection to looking pathetic. Besides, they are always under the impression that the artist is laughing at them. It is a sad fact, but there is no doubt that the poor are completely unconscious of their own picturesqueness. Those of them who can be induced to sit do so with the idea that the artist is merely a benevolent philanthropist who has chosen an eccentric method of distributing alms to the undeserving. Perhaps the School Board will teach the London gamin his own artistic value, and then they will be better models than they are now. One remarkable privilege belongs to the Academy model, that of extorting a sovereign from any newly elected Associate or R.A. They wait at Burlington House till the announcement is made, and then race to the hapless artist's house. The one who arrives first receives the money. They have of late been much troubled at the long distances they have had to run, and they look with disfavour on the election of artists who live at Hampstead or at Bedford Park, for it is considered a point of honour not to employ the underground railway, omnibuses, or any artificial means of locomotion. The race is to the swift.

Besides the professional posers of the studio there are posers of the Row, the posers at afternoon teas, the posers in politics and the circus posers. All four classes are delightful, but only the last class is ever really decorative. Acrobats and gymnasts can give the young painter infinite suggestions, for they bring into their art an element of swiftness of motion and of constant change that the studio model necessarily lacks. What is interesting in these 'slaves of the ring' is that with them Beauty is an unconscious result not a conscious aim, the result in fact of the mathematical calculation of curves and distances, of absolute precision of eye, of the scientific knowledge of the equilibrium of forces, and of perfect physical training. A good acrobat is always graceful, though grace is never his object; he is graceful because he does what he has to do in the best way in which it can be done—graceful because he is natural. If an ancient Greek were to come to life now, which considering the probable severity of his criticisms would be rather trying to our conceit, he would be found far oftener at the circus than at the theatre. A good circus is an oasis of Hellenism in a world that reads too much to be wise, and thinks too much to be beautiful. If it were not for the running-ground at Eton, the towing-path at Oxford, the Thames swimming-baths, and the yearly circuses, humanity would forget the plastic perfection of its own form, and degenerate into a race of short-sighted professors and spectacled précieuses. Not that the circus proprietors are, as a rule, conscious of their high mission. Do they not bore us with the haute école, and weary us with Shakespearean clowns? Still, at least, they give us acrobats, and the acrobat is an artist. The mere fact that he never speaks to the audience shows how well he appreciates the great truth that the aim of art is not to reveal personality but to please. The clown may be blatant, but the acrobat is always beautiful. He is an interesting combination of the spirit of Greek sculpture with the spangles of the modern costumier. He has even had his niche in the novels of our age, and if Manette Salomon be the unmasking of the model, Les Frères Zemganno is the apotheosis of the acrobat.

As regards the influence of the ordinary model on our English school of painting, it cannot be said that it is altogether good. It is, of course, an advantage for the young artist sitting in his studio to be able to isolate 'a little corner of life,' as the French say, from disturbing surroundings, and to study it under certain effects of light and shade. But this very isolation leads often to mere mannerism in the painter, and robs him of that broad acceptance of the general facts of life which is the very essence of art. Model-painting, in a word, while it may be the condition of art, is not by any means its aim.

It is simply practice, not perfection. Its use trains the eye and the hand of the painter, its abuse produces in his work an effect of mere posing and prettiness. It is the secret of much of the artificiality of modern art, this constant posing of pretty people, and when art becomes artificial it becomes monotonous. Outside the little world of the studio, with its draperies and its bric-à-brac, lies the world of life with its infinite, its Shakespearean variety. We must, however, distinguish between the two kinds of models, those who sit for the figure and those who sit for the costume. The study of the first is always excellent, but the costume-model is becoming rather wearisome in modern pictures. It is really of very little use to dress up a London girl in Greek draperies and to paint her as a goddess. The robe may be the robe of Athens, but the face is usually the face of Brompton. Now and then, it is true, one comes across a model whose face is an exquisite anachronism, and who looks lovely and natural in the dress of any century but her own. This, however, is rather rare. As a rule models are absolutely de notre siècle, and should be painted as such. Unfortunately they are not, and, as a consequence, we are shown every year a series of scenes from fancy dress balls which are called historical pictures, but are little more than mediocre representations of modern people masquerading. In France they are wiser. The French painter uses the model simply for study; for the finished picture he goes direct to life.

However, we must not blame the sitters for the shortcomings of the artists. The English models are a well-behaved and hard-working class, and if they are more interested in artists than in art, a large section of the public is in the same condition, and most of our modern exhibitions seem to justify its choice.

POEMS IN PROSE

Fortnight Review, July 1894.

The Artist

One evening there came into his soul the desire to fashion an image of *The Pleasure that abideth for a Moment*. And he went forth into the world to look for bronze. For he could think only in bronze.

But all the bronze of the whole world had disappeared, nor anywhere in the whole world was there any bronze to be found, save only the bronze of the image of *The Sorrow that endureth for Ever*.

Now this image he had himself, and with his own hands, fashioned, and had set it on the tomb of the one thing he had loved in life. On the tomb of the dead thing he had most loved had he set this image of his own fashioning, that it might serve as a sign of the love of man that dieth not, and a symbol of the sorrow of man that endureth for ever. And in the whole world there was no other bronze save the bronze of this image.

And he took the image he had fashioned, and set it in a great furnace, and gave it to the fire.

And out of the bronze of the image of *The Sorrow that endureth for Ever* he fashioned an image of *The Pleasure that abideth for a Moment*.

The Doer of Good

It was night-time and He was alone.

And He saw afar-off the walls of a round city and went towards the city.

And when He came near He heard within the city the tread of the feet of joy, and the laughter of the mouth of gladness and the loud noise of many lutes. And He knocked at the gate and certain of the gate-keepers opened to Him.

And He beheld a house that was of marble and had fair pillars of marble before it. The pillars were hung with garlands, and within and without there were torches of cedar. And He entered the house.

And when He had passed through the hall of chalcedony and the hall of jasper, and reached the long hall of feasting, He saw lying on a couch of sea-purple one whose hair was crowned with red roses and whose lips were red with wine.

And He went behind him and touched him on the shoulder and said to him, 'Why do you live like this?'

And the young man turned round and recognised Him, and made answer and said, 'But I was a leper once, and you healed me. How else should I live?'

And He passed out of the house and went again into the street.

And after a little while He saw one whose face and raiment were painted and whose feet were shod with pearls. And behind her came, slowly as a hunter, a young man who wore a cloak of two colours. Now the face of the woman was as the fair face of an idol, and the eyes of the young man were bright with lust.

And He followed swiftly and touched the hand of the young man and said to him, 'Why do you look at this woman and in such wise?'

And the young man turned round and recognised Him and said, 'But I was blind once, and you gave me sight. At what else should I look?'

And He ran forward and touched the painted raiment of the woman and said to her, 'Is there no other way in which to walk save the way of sin?'

And the woman turned round and recognised Him, and laughed and said, 'But you forgave me my sins, and the way is a pleasant way.'

And He passed out of the city.

And when He had passed out of the city He saw seated by the roadside a young man who was weeping.

And He went towards him and touched the long locks of his hair and said to him, 'Why are you weeping?'

And the young man looked up and recognised Him and made answer, 'But I was dead once, and you raised me from the dead. What else should I do but weep?'

The Disciple

When Narcissus died the pool of his pleasure changed from a cup of sweet waters into a cup of salt tears, and the Oreads came weeping through the woodland that they might sing to the pool and give it comfort.

And when they saw that the pool had changed from a cup of sweet waters into a cup of salt tears, they loosened the green tresses of their hair and cried to the pool and said, 'We do not wonder that you should mourn in this manner for Narcissus, so beautiful was he.'

'But was Narcissus beautiful?' said the pool.

'Who should know that better than you?' answered the Oreads. 'Us did he ever pass by, but you he sought for, and would lie on your banks and look down at you, and in the mirror of your waters he would mirror his own beauty.'

And the pool answered, 'But I loved Narcissus because, as he lay on my banks and looked down at me, in the mirror of his eyes I saw ever my own beauty mirrored.'

The Master

Now when the darkness came over the earth Joseph of Arimathea, having lighted a torch of pinewood, passed down from the hill into the valley. For he had business in his own home.

And kneeling on the flint stones of the Valley of Desolation he saw a young man who was naked and weeping. His hair was the colour of honey, and his body was as a white flower, but he had wounded his body with thorns and on his hair had he set ashes as a crown.

And he who had great possessions said to the young man who was naked and weeping, 'I do not wonder that your sorrow is so great, for surely He was a just man.'

And the young man answered, 'It is not for Him that I am weeping, but for myself. I too have changed water into wine, and I have healed the leper and given sight to the blind. I have walked upon the waters, and from the dwellers in the tombs I have cast out devils. I have fed the hungry in the desert where there was no food, and I have raised the dead from their narrow houses, and at my bidding, and before a great multitude, of people, a barren fig-tree withered away. All things that this man has done I have done also. And yet they have not crucified me.'

The House of Judgment

And there was silence in the House of Judgment, and the Man came naked before God.

And God opened the Book of the Life of the Man.

And God said to the Man, 'Thy life hath been evil, and thou hast shown cruelty to those who were in need of succour, and to those who lacked help thou hast been bitter and hard of heart. The poor called to thee and thou didst not hearken, and thine ears were closed to the cry of My afflicted. The inheritance of the fatherless thou didst take unto thyself, and thou didst send the foxes into the vineyard of thy neighbour's field. Thou didst take the bread of the children and give it to the dogs to eat, and My lepers who lived in the marshes, and were at peace and praised Me, thou didst drive forth on to the highways, and on Mine earth out of which I made thee thou didst spill innocent blood.'

And the Man made answer and said, 'Even so did I.'

And again God opened the Book of the Life of the Man.

And God said to the Man, 'Thy life hath been evil, and the Beauty I have shown thou hast sought for, and the Good I have hidden thou didst pass by. The walls of thy chamber were painted with images, and from the bed of thine abominations thou didst rise up to the sound of flutes. Thou didst build seven altars to the sins I have suffered, and didst eat of the thing that may not be eaten, and the purple of thy raiment was broidered with the three signs of shame. Thine idols were neither of gold nor of silver that endure, but of flesh that dieth. Thou didst stain their hair with perfumes and put pomegranates in their hands. Thou didst stain their feet with saffron and spread carpets before them. With antimony thou didst stain their eyelids and their bodies thou didst smear with myrrh. Thou didst bow thyself to the ground before them, and the thrones of thine idols were set in the sun. Thou didst show to the sun thy shame and to the moon thy madness.'

And the Man made answer and said, 'Even so did I.'

And a third time God opened the Book of the Life of the Man.

And God said to the Man, 'Evil hath been thy life, and with evil didst thou requite good, and with wrongdoing kindness. The hands that fed thee thou didst wound, and the breasts that gave thee suck thou didst despise. He who came to thee with water went away thirsting, and the outlawed men who hid thee in their tents at night thou didst betray before dawn. Thine enemy who spared thee thou didst snare in an ambush, and the friend who walked with thee thou didst sell for a price, and to those who brought thee Love thou didst ever give Lust in thy turn.'

And the Man made answer and said, 'Even so did I.'

And God closed the Book of the Life of the Man, and said, 'Surely I will send thee into Hell. Even into Hell will I send thee.'

And the Man cried out, 'Thou canst not.'

And God said to the Man, 'Wherefore can I not send thee to Hell, and for what reason?'

'Because in Hell have I always lived,' answered the Man.

And there was silence in the House of Judgment.

And after a space God spake, and said to the Man, 'Seeing that I may not send thee into Hell, surely I will send thee unto Heaven. Even unto Heaven will I send thee.'

And the Man cried out, 'Thou canst not.'

And God said to the Man, 'Wherefore can I not send thee unto Heaven, and for what reason?'

'Because never, and in no place, have I been able to imagine it,' answered the Man.

And there was silence in the House of Judgment.

The Teacher of Wisdom

From his childhood he had been as one filled with the perfect knowledge of God, and even while he was yet but a lad many of the saints, as well as certain holy women who dwelt in the free city of his birth, had been stirred to much wonder by the grave wisdom of his answers.

And when his parents had given him the robe and the ring of manhood he kissed them, and left them and went out into the world, that he might speak to the world about God. For there were at that time many in the world who either knew not God at all, or had but an incomplete knowledge of Him, or worshipped the false gods who dwell in groves and have no care of their worshippers.

And he set his face to the sun and journeyed, walking without sandals, as he had seen the saints walk, and carrying at his girdle a leathern wallet and a little water-bottle of burnt clay.

And as he walked along the highway he was full of the joy that comes from the perfect knowledge of God, and he sang praises unto God without ceasing; and after a time he reached a strange land in which there were many cities.

And he passed through eleven cities. And some of these cities were in valleys, and others were by the banks of great rivers, and others were set on hills. And in each city he found a disciple who loved him and followed him, and a great multitude also of people followed him from each city, and the knowledge of God spread in the whole land, and many of the rulers were converted, and the priests of the temples in which there were idols found that half of their gain was gone, and when they beat upon their drums at noon none, or but a few, came with peacocks and with offerings of flesh as had been the custom of the land before his coming.

Yet the more the people followed him, and the greater the number of his disciples, the greater became his sorrow. And he knew not why his sorrow was so great. For he spake ever about God, and out of the fulness of that perfect knowledge of God which God had Himself given to him.

And one evening he passed out of the eleventh city, which was a city of Armenia, and his disciples and a great crowd of people followed after him; and he went up on to a mountain and sat down on a rock that was on the mountain, and his disciples stood round him, and the multitude knelt in the valley.

And he bowed his head on his hands and wept, and said to his Soul, 'Why is it that I am full of sorrow and fear, and that each of my disciples is an enemy that walks in the noonday?' And his Soul answered him and said, 'God filled thee with the perfect knowledge of Himself, and thou hast given this knowledge away to others. The pearl of great price thou hast divided, and the vesture without seam thou hast parted asunder. He who giveth away wisdom robbeth himself. He is as one who giveth his treasure to a robber. Is not God wiser than thou art? Who art thou to give away the secret that God hath told thee? I was rich once, and thou hast made me poor. Once I saw God, and now thou hast hidden Him from me.'

And he wept again, for he knew that his Soul spake truth to him, and that he had given to others the perfect knowledge of God, and that he was as one clinging to the skirts of God, and that his faith was leaving him by reason of the number of those who believed in him.

And he said to himself, 'I will talk no more about God. He who giveth away wisdom robbeth himself.'

And after the space of some hours his disciples came near him and bowed themselves to the ground and said, 'Master, talk to us about God, for thou hast the perfect knowledge of God, and no man save thee hath this knowledge.'

And he answered them and said, 'I will talk to you about all other things that are in heaven and on earth, but about God I will not talk to you. Neither now, nor at any time, will I talk to you about God.'

And they were wroth with him and said to him, 'Thou hast led us into the desert that we might hearken to thee. Wilt thou send us away hungry, and the great multitude that thou hast made to follow thee?'

And he answered them and said, 'I will not talk to you about God.'

And the multitude murmured against him and said to him, 'Thou hast led us into the desert, and hast given us no food to eat. Talk to us about God and it will suffice us.'

But he answered them not a word. For he knew that if he spake to them about God he would give away his treasure.

And his disciples went away sadly, and the multitude of people returned to their own homes. And many died on the way.

And when he was alone he rose up and set his face to the moon, and journeyed for seven moons, speaking to no man nor making any answer. And when the seventh moon had waned he reached that desert which is the desert of the Great River. And having found a cavern in which a Centaur had once dwelt, he took it for his place of dwelling, and made himself a mat of reeds on which to lie, and became a hermit. And every hour the Hermit praised God that He had suffered him to keep some knowledge of Him and of His wonderful greatness.

Now, one evening, as the Hermit was seated before the cavern in which he had made his place of dwelling, he beheld a young man of evil and beautiful face who passed by in mean apparel and with empty hands. Every evening with empty hands the young man passed by, and every morning he returned with his hands full of purple and pearls. For he was a Robber and robbed the caravans of the merchants.

And the Hermit looked at him and pitied him. But he spake not a word. For he knew that he who speaks a word loses his faith.

And one morning, as the young man returned with his hands full of purple and pearls, he stopped and frowned and stamped his foot upon the sand, and said to the Hermit: 'Why do you look at me ever in this manner as I pass by? What is it that I see in your eyes? For no man has looked at me before in this manner. And the thing is a thorn and a trouble to me.'

And the Hermit answered him and said, 'What you see in my eyes is pity. Pity is what looks out at you from my eyes.'

And the young man laughed with scorn, and cried to the Hermit in a bitter voice, and said to him, 'I have purple and pearls in my hands, and you have but a mat of reeds on which to lie. What pity should you have for me? And for what reason have you this pity?'

'I have pity for you,' said the Hermit, 'because you have no knowledge of God.'

'Is this knowledge of God a precious thing?' asked the young man, and he came close to the mouth of the cavern.

'It is more precious than all the purple and the pearls of the world,' answered the Hermit.

'And have you got it?' said the young Robber, and he came closer still.

'Once, indeed,' answered the Hermit, 'I possessed the perfect knowledge of God. But in my foolishness I parted with it, and divided it amongst others. Yet even now is such knowledge as remains to me more precious than purple or pearls.'

And when the young Robber heard this he threw away the purple and the pearls that he was bearing in his hands, and drawing a sharp sword of curved steel he said to the Hermit, 'Give me, forthwith this knowledge of God that you possess, or I will surely slay you. Wherefore should I not slay him who has a treasure greater than my treasure?'

And the Hermit spread out his arms and said, 'Were it not better for me to go unto the uttermost courts of God and praise Him, than to live in the world and have no knowledge of Him? Slay me if that be your desire. But I will not give away my knowledge of God.'

And the young Robber knelt down and besought him, but the Hermit would not talk to him about God, nor give him his Treasure, and the young Robber rose up and said to the Hermit, 'Be it as you will. As for myself, I will go to the City of the Seven Sins, that is but three days' journey from this place, and for my purple they will give me pleasure, and for my pearls they will sell me joy.' And he took up the purple and the pearls and went swiftly away.

And the Hermit cried out and followed him and besought him. For the space of three days he followed the young Robber on the road and entreated him to return, nor to enter into the City of the Seven Sins.

And ever and anon the young Robber looked back at the Hermit and called to him, and said, 'Will you give me this knowledge of God which is more precious than purple and pearls? If you will give me that, I will not enter the city.'

And ever did the Hermit answer, 'All things that I have I will give thee, save that one thing only. For that thing it is not lawful for me to give away.'

And in the twilight of the third day they came nigh to the great scarlet gates of the City of the Seven Sins. And from the city there came the sound of much laughter.

And the young Robber laughed in answer, and sought to knock at the gate. And as he did so the Hermit ran forward and caught him by the skirts of his raiment, and said to him: 'Stretch forth your hands, and set your arms around my neck, and put your ear close to my lips, and I will give you what remains to me of the knowledge of God.' And the young Robber stopped.

And when the Hermit had given away his knowledge of God, he fell upon the ground and wept, and a great darkness hid from him the city and the young Robber, so that he saw them no more.

And as he lay there weeping he was ware of One who was standing beside him; and He who was standing beside him had feet of brass and hair like fine wool. And He raised the Hermit up, and said to him: 'Before this time thou hadst the perfect knowledge of God. Now thou shalt have the perfect love of God. Wherefore art thou weeping?' And he kissed him.

FOOTNOTES

[29] Plato's *Laws; Æschylus' Prometheus Bound.*

[31] Somewhat in the same spirit Plato, in his Laws, appeals to the local position of Ilion among the rivers of the plain, as a proof that it was not built till long after the Deluge.

[32] Plutarch remarks that the only evidence Greece possesses of the truth that the legendary power of Athens is no 'romance or idle story,' is the public and sacred buildings. This is an instance of the exaggerated importance given to ruins against which Thucydides is warning us.

[37] The fictitious sale in the Roman marriage *per coemptionem* was originally, of course, a real sale.

[43] Notably, of course, in the case of heat and its laws.

[57] Cousin errs a good deal in this respect. To say, as he did, 'Give me the latitude and the longitude of a country, its rivers and its mountains, and I will deduce the race,' is surely a glaring exaggeration.

[59] The monarchical, aristocratical, and democratic elements of the Roman constitution are referred to.

[63a] Polybius, vi. 9. αὕτη πολιτειῶν ἀνακύκλωσις, αὕτς φύσεως οἰκονομία.

[63b] χωρὶς ὀργῆς ἢ φθόνου ποιούμεηος τὴν ἀπόφασιν.

[63c] The various stages are σύστασις, αὔξησις, ἀκμή, μεταβολὴ ἐις τοὔμπαλιν.

[68] Polybius, xii. 24.

[69a] Polybius, i. 4, viii. 4, specially; and really passim.

[69b] He makes one exception.

[69c] Polybius, viii. 4.

[71] Polybius, xvi. 12.

[72a] Polybius, viii. 4: τὸ παραδοξάτον καθ' ἡμᾶς ἔργον ἡ τύχη συνετέλεσε; τοῦτο δ' ἔστι τὸ πάντα τὰ γνωριζόμενα μέρη τῆς οἰκουμένης ὑπὸ μίαν ἀρχὴν καὶ δυναστείαν ἀγαγεῖν, ὃ πρότερον οὐχ εὑρίσκεται γεγονός.

[72b] Polybius resembled Gibbon in many respects. Like him he held that all religions were to the philosopher equally false, to the vulgar equally true, to the statesman equally useful.

[76] Cf. Polybius, xii. 25, ἐπεὶ ψιλῶς λεγόμενον αὐτὸ γεγονὸς ψυχαγωγεῖ μέν, ὠφελεῖ δ' οὐδέν· προστεθείσης δὲ τῆς αἰτίας ἔγκαρπος ἡ τῆς ἱστορίας γίγνεται χρῆσις.

[78] Polybius, xxii. 8.

[81] I mean particularly as regards his sweeping denunciation of the complete moral decadence of Greek society during the Peloponnesain War, which, from what remains to us of Athenian literature, we know must have been completely exaggerated. Or, rather, he is looking at men merely in their political dealings: and in politics the man who is personally honourable and refined will not scruple to do anything for his party.

[86] Polybius, xii. 25.

[124] As an instance of the inaccuracy of published reports of this lecture, it may be mentioned that all unauthorised versions give this passage as *The artist may trace the depressed revolution of Bunthorne simply to the lack of technical means!*

[206] *The Two Paths*, Lect. iii. p. 123 (1859 ed.).

FOR LOVE OF THE KING

INTRODUCTORY NOTE

The very interesting and richly coloured masque or pantomimic play which is here printed in book form for the first time, was invented sometime in 1894 or possibly a little earlier. It was written, not for publication, but as a personal gift to the author's friend and friend of his family, Mrs. Chan Toon, and was sent to her with the letter that follows and explains its origin.

Mrs. Chan Toon, before her marriage to Mr. Chan Toon, a Burmese gentleman, nephew of the King of Burma and a barrister of the Middle Temple, was Miss Mabel Cosgrove, the daughter of Mr. Ernest Cosgrove of Lancaster Gate, a friend of Sir William and Lady Wilde, and herself brought up with Oscar and his brother Willie.

For a long while Mrs. Chan Toon, who after her husband's death became Mrs. Woodhouse-Pearse, refused to permit the masque to be printed. The late Robert Ross much wanted to include it in an edition of Wilde's works, of which it now forms a part, but he could not obtain its owner's consent. An arrangement, however, having been completed, the play is now made public.

TITE STREET, CHELSEA,

November 27, 1894

My dear Mrs. Chan Toon,

I am greatly repentant being so long in acknowledging receipt of "Told on the Pagoda." I enjoyed reading the stories, and much admired their quaint and delicate charm. Burmah calls to me.

Under another cover I am sending you a fairy play entitled "For Love of the King," just for your own amusement. It is the outcome of long and luminous talks with your distinguished husband in the Temple and on the river, in the days when I was meditating writing a novel as beautiful and as intricate as a Persian praying-rug. I hope that I have caught the atmosphere.

I should like to see it acted in your Garden House on some night when the sky is a sheet of violet and the stars like women's eyes. Alas, it is not likely.

I am in the throes of a new comedy. I met a perfectly wonderful person the other day who unconsciously has irradiated my present with sinuous suggestion: a Swedish Baron, French in manner, Athenian in mind, and Oriental in morals. His society is a series of revelations. . . .

I was at Oakley Street on Thursday; my mother tells me she sends you a letter nearly every week.

Constance desires to be warmly remembered, while I, who am bathing my brow in the perfume of water-lilies, lay myself at the feet of you and yours.

OSCAR WILDE

PRINCIPAL CHARACTERS OF THE PLAY

KING MENG BENG (*Lord of a Thousand White Elephants, Countless Umbrellas and other attributes of greatness*).

U. RAI GYAN THOO (*A Prime Minister*).

SHAH MAH PHRU (*A Girl, half Italian, half Burmese, of dazzling beauty*).

DHAMMATHAT (*Legal Adviser to the Court*).

HIP LOONG (*A Chinese Wizard of great repute*).

MOUNG PHO MHIN (*Minister of Finance*).

TWO ENVOYS FROM THE KING OF CEYLON.

NOBLES, COURTIERS, SOOTHSAYERS, POONYGEES, DANCING GIRLS, BETEL-NUT CARRIERS, UMBRELLA BEARERS, FOLLOWERS, SERVANTS, SLAVES, amongst whom are several CHINESE but no INDIANS.

TIME: *The Sixteenth Century.*

ACT I

SCENE I

The palace of the king of burmah. The scene is laid in the Hall of a Hundred Doors. In the distance can be seen the moat, the waiting elephants, and the peacocks promenading proudly in the blinding sunshine of late afternoon. The scene discovers king meng beng seated on a raised cushion sewn with rubies, under a canopy supported by four attendants, motionless as bronze figures. By his side is a betel-nut box, glittering with gems. On either side of him, but much lower down, are the two ambassadors of the king of ceylon, bearers of the King of Ceylon's consent to the marriage of his only daughter to Meng Beng in two years' time, men of grave, majestic mien, clad in flowing robes almost monastic in their white simplicity. They smoke gravely at the invitation of meng beng.

Round about are grouped the courtiers, the poonygees, and the kneeling servants, while in the background wait the dancing girls. Banners, propelled with a measured rhythm, create an agreeable breeze. On a great table of gold stand goblets of gold and heaped-up fruits. Everywhere will be observed the emblems of the Royal Peacock and the Sacred White Elephant. Burmese musical instruments sound an abrupt but charming discord. The poinsettias flower punctuates points of deepest colour from out of vases fashioned like the lotus. Orchids are everywhere. The indescribable scent of Burmah steals across the footlights. The glow, the colour, the sun-swept vista sweeps across the senses. the king claps his hands. The dancing girls, at the signal, advance. They are clad in dresses made of fish scales, which are fastened with diamonds and pale emeralds, to imitate the upthrown spray on the crest of a wave. The dance concluded, the cingalese ambassadors rise and prepare to take ceremonious leave of the king, who hands to them, through his vizier, his message to His Majesty of Ceylon, inscribed on palm leaves and enclosed in a bejewelled casket.

Many flowery speeches pass. Exit (L.), walking backwards.

the king expresses a desire for rest before starting by the Moon of Taboung [4] for the Pagoda of Golden Flowers.

Exit meng beng (C.), an alcove of satin hangings which commands a view of the great hall.

The Crowd break up into groups. u. rai gyan thoo and moung pho mhin converse on the tendency of the King to interference in affairs of State; his extreme youth and delicacy of temperament; the pity that the marriage is to be so long delayed; the necessity to find him some distraction in the meantime.

Suddenly the tom-toms sound loudly. There is much movement. The moon rises over the sea. Torches flare as the attendants move to and fro in the gardens beyond.

The White Elephant of the King, with its trappings of gold, is led to the entrance where, at a word, it sinks obediently to the ground.

the king appears. He has changed his gay apple-green dress to one of more sombre hue. He enters the howdah—the elephant rises—the procession starts. It consists of not fewer than two hundred persons, keeping in view of the audience until lost by a bend in the avenue.

SCENE II

THE PAGODA OF GOLDEN FLOWERS

Midnight

Surrounded by Peepul-trees, the great Htee, [6] with its crown of a myriad jewels, rises towards the violet, star-studded sky, its golden bells tinkling in a soft night-wind.

When the curtain rises, the circular platform is deserted. Statues of Buddha seated and recumbent fill the numberless niches in the wall, and before each burn long candles; heaped-up pink roses and japonica on brass trays are lit from above by swinging coloured lamps. At intervals are stalls laden with fruit and cheroots. All is mysterious, solemn, beautiful.

A deep Burmese gong tolls. People emerge from the four staircases that lead up to the platform. Men, women, and children, all in gala attire. The young people conversing, gesticulating, smiling. The older people, more subdued, carry beads and votive offering to Buddha. Charming Burmese girls, with huge cigars, meet and greet handsome Burmese men smoking cheroots and wearing flowers in their ears. Children play silently with coloured balls. In the corners, under canopies, are seated fortune-tellers, busy casting horoscopes. It is a veritable riot of colour, with never a discordant note.

Through the crowd the king passes alone and unrecognised, and disappears through double doors of heavily carved teak wood. He has hardly passed when mah phru, a very lovely girl, enters in distress. She whispers that she desires an audience of the King who has come amongst them. The few who hear her shrug their shoulders, smile, and pass on. They are incredulous. She goes from group to group, but the people turn from her with disdain. Then the great doors open, and the king is seen. The girl throws herself, Oriental fashion, in his path. Her beauty and her pathos arrest his attention and he waves aside those who would interfere. She implores the king's protection. She is willing to be his slave. He listens with deep attention. She explains that since her father's death she has been continuously persecuted by the village people on the double count of her Italian blood and her poverty.

The girl invites him to come to her hut in the forest and verify what she says. With a gesture he signifies that he will follow where she leads. She rises. The crowd gathers round—all are hushed to silence. the king, as one entranced, puts aside all who would in any way interfere. The girl precedes him, going from the Pagoda towards the night. When she reaches the great staircase, she beckons, Oriental fashion, with downward hand. The scene should, in grouping and colour, make for rare beauty.

SCENE III

A humble dhunni-thatched hut, set amidst the whispering grandeur of the jungle, with its mighty trees, its trackless paths, its indescribable silence. The curtain discovers mah phru and the king, who expresses his amazement at the loneliness and the poverty of her lot. She explains that poverty is not what frightens her, but the enmity of those who live yonder, and who make it almost impossible for her to sell her cucumbers or her pineapples. the king's gaze never leaves the face or figure of the girl. He declares that he will protect her—that he will build her a home here in the shadow of the loneliness around them. He has two years of an unfettered freedom—for those years he can command his life. He loves her, he desires her—they will find a Paradise together. The girl trembles with joy—with fear—with surprise. "And after two years?" she asks. "Death," he answers.

ACT II

SCENE I

The jungle once more. Time: noonday. In place of the hut is a building, half Burmese, half Italian villa, of white Chunam, with curled roofs rising on roofs, gilded and adorned with spiral carvings and a myriad golden and jewel-encrusted bells. On the broad verandahs are thrown Eastern carpets, rugs, embroideries.

The world is sun-soaked. The surrounding trees stand sentinel-like in the burning light. Burmese servants squat motionless, smoking on the broad white steps that lead from the house to the garden. The crows croak drowsily at intervals. Parrots scream intermittently. The sound of a guitar playing a Venetian love-song can be heard coming from the interior. Otherwise life apparently sleeps. Two elderly retainers break the silence.

"When will the Thakin tire of this?" one asks the other in kindly contempt.

"The end is already at hand. I read it at dawn to-day."

"Whence will it come?"

"I know not. It is written that one heart will break."

"He will leave her?"

"He will leave her. He will have no choice—who can war with Fate?"

The sun shifts a little; a light breeze kisses the motionless palm leaves— they quiver gracefully. Attendants appear R. and L. bearing a great Shamiana (tent), silver poles, carved chairs, foot supports, fruit, flowers, embroidered fans. Three musicians in semi-Venetian-Burmese costume follow with their instruments. The tent erected, enter (C.) meng beng and mah phru, followed by two Burmese women carrying two tiny children in Burmese fashion on their hips.

The servants retire to a distance. meng beng and mah phru seat themselves on carven chairs; the children are placed at their feet and given coloured glass balls to play with. meng beng and mah phru gaze at them with deep affection and then at each other.

The musicians play light, zephyr-like airs. meng beng and mah phru talk together. meng beng smokes a cigar, mah phru has one of the big yellow cheroots affected by Burmese women to-day.

"It wants but two days to the two years," he tells her sadly.

"And you are happy?"

"As a god."

She smiles radiantly. She suspects nothing. She is more beautiful than before. Her dress is of the richest Mandalay silks. She wears big nadoungs of rubies in her ears.

Presently meng beng arranges a set of ivory chessmen on a low table between them. The sun sinks slowly. The sound of approaching wheels is heard.

Enter (C.) u. rai gyan thoo, preceded by two servants. meng beng looks up in surprise—in alarm. He rises, etc., and goes forward. u. rai gyan thoo presents a letter written on palm leaves. meng beng does not open it.

The curtains at the opening of the tent are, Oriental fashion, dropped. The music ceases.

meng beng and the grand vizier converse apart. The Minister explains that the Princess of Ceylon's ship and its great convoy have already been sighted. The Court and city wait in eager expectancy. The King has worshipped long enough at the Pagoda of Golden Flowers—his subjects and his bride call to him. u. rai gyan thoo has come to take him to them.

meng beng is terribly distressed.

"You can return one day," the Vizier tells him. "The Pagoda will remain. I also, once, in years long dead, Lord of the Sea and Moon, worshipped at a Pagoda."

meng beng seeks mah phru to explain that he goes on urgent affairs, that he will come back to her and to his sons, perhaps before the waning of the new moon. Their parting is sad with the pensive sadness of look and gesture peculiar to Eastern people.

meng beng goes (C.) with u. rai gyan thoo. mah phru mounts to the verandah to watch them go from behind the curtains. Then, slowly sinking across the heaped-up cushions, she faints.

The sun has set. The music ceases. The melancholy cry of the peacocks fills the silence.

ACT DROP

ACT III

SCENE I

Seven years have elapsed.

The same scene.

Curtain discovers mah phru seated on a high verandah. A clearance has been made in the surrounding trees to give a full view of the road beyond. She is watching, always watching. With her are two beautiful little boys.

"To-day, perhaps," she murmurs. "Perhaps to-morrow; but without fail—one day."

"Look!" she cries. "At last my lord returns!"

Coming up the jungle road, in view of the audience, are a bevy of horsemen.

mah phru, wondering, descends to greet them. Enter u. rai gyan thoo. He is dressed all in white, which is Burmese mourning. mah phru sinks back—she fears the worst. The old man reassures her. He tells her that meng beng has sent for his sons—that the Queen is dead, and there is no heir.

"Queen? What Queen?" demands mah phru.

"The Queen of Burmah."

So mah phru learns for the first time that her lover is the ruler of the country, supreme master of and dictator to everyone.

Weeping, but not daring to disobey, she summons the children to her; then, sinking on her knees, entreats in moving and pathetic words to be permitted to go with them, in the lowest most menial capacity. u. rai gyan thoo refuses. There is no place for her in the greatness of the world yonder.

"Even Kings forget," he says. "It is the command of the supreme Lord of the Earth and of the Sky that she remain where she is."

Then he orders his followers to make the necessary arrangements for the safe journey of their future king and his brother.

The children stand passive in their gay dress, but are bewildered and afraid.

mah phru has risen to her feet. She appears as if turned to bronze—a model of restraint and dignity, blent with colour and beauty and infinite grace.

THE CURTAIN DESCENDS SLOWLY

<u>SCENE II</u>

The same night.

The home of the Chinese Wizard, hip loong, by the river—a place fitted with Chinese things: Dragons of gold with eyes of jade gleaming from out dim corners, Buddhas of gigantic size fashioned of priceless metals with heads that move, swinging banners with fringes of many-coloured stones, lanterns with glass slides on which are painted grotesque figures. The air is full of the scent of joss sticks. The Wizard reclines on a divan, inhaling opium slowly, clothed with the subdued gorgeousness of China—blue and tomato-red predominate. He has the appearance of a wrinkled walnut. His forehead is a lattice-work of wrinkles. His pigtail, braided with red, is twisted round his head. His hands are as claws. The effect is weird, unearthly.

Enter mah phru.

The Wizard silently motions her to some piled-up cushions at a little distance. He listens to what she tells him. He appears unmoved, at a recital apparently full of tragedy. Only the eyes of the dragons move, and the heads of the Buddhas go slowly like pendulums. When she has finished speaking, hip loong makes reply.

"This is how passion always ends. I have lived for a thousand years; and on this planet it is ever the same."

mah phru is not listening.

"How can I go to my children?" she demands, once again.

"I can turn you into a bird," the Wizard says. "You can fly to the palace and walk and watch ever on that terrace in the rose gardens above the sea."

"What bird?" she asks, trembling.

"You shall have the form of the white paddy bird, because, though a woman and foolish as women ever are, you are very pure ivory. O! daughter of man and of love."

To this mah phru dissents. She paces the long room.

"Transform me into a peacock; they are more beautiful."

The Wizard, leaning on his elbow, smiles, and the smile is a revelation of a mocking comprehension.

"So be it." He bows his head.

The lights fade one by one.

CURTAIN

SCENE III

The Gardens of the Palace of the King.

Time: late afternoon.

Colonnades of roses stretch away on every side. Fountains play, throwing a shower on water-lilies of monstrous size. Peacocks walk with stately tread across the green turf. Only one, larger and more beautiful than the rest, is perched alone, with drooping head and folded tail, on the broad-pillared terrace that overhangs the sea. The scene is aglow with light and colour, yet holds a shadowed silence.

Enter some courtiers, who converse in perturbed fashion as they go towards the Palace.

Enter moung pho mhin and u. rai gyan thoo, accompanied by the

Court Physicians and Astrologers.

"The King cannot live beyond the night," the Physicians say. The sudden, mysterious illness that has attacked him defies their skill.

The Astrologers declare that the stars in their courses fight against his recovery; unless a miracle should happen, the new day will see him dead.

The Ministers regard each other in consternation; then walk the terrace with bent heads.

The peacock on the wall spreads its tail and utters a melancholy cry of poignant pain.

The listeners start in superstitious horror.

The peacock folds its tail and resumes its meditations.

"That bird is not as other birds," one astrologer declares. "I have watched it for years past—it is ever alone—the others all avoid it. I think it has a soul."

"You mistake," replies his colleague; "it is but an evil Nat. [32] Observe its eyes: they are not those of a bird; they are those of a spirit in prison."

They pass on in the wake of the ministers.

The peacock closes its eyes.

Enter the two young princes, accompanied by two great Pegu hounds. They converse in subdued tones, strolling slowly. They are followed by pages of honour, carrying grain, which the young men proceed to distribute amongst the birds as they rapidly approach them. The peacock on the wall never stirs; she watches the young men always. Then the elder one comes with a handful of food and proffers it, but the peacock does not eat.

"I shall never understand you, Queen of the Kingdom of Birds," he says, and strokes her feathers. At his touch the plumage scintillates with a brighter, a more exquisite sheen.

He murmurs to the bird in soft tones and mythical words. He tells it that the fear of everyone is that the King is mortally stricken, for he lies yonder in most strange and evil agony; that the hearts of himself and his brother are numb with the sorrow that knows no language. The bird listens eagerly. And if the King should go, he, the speaker, will reign in his stead. The prospect fills him with fear. He desires, as also his brother, if the King must die, to return to dwell in the forest with the mother who he knows awaits them there.

The peacock spreads its wings as if for flight, then crouches down once more, and over it watches the young prince.

The sun envelops them both in a sudden shaft of rose and purple and gold. A servant descends and comes across the grass. He shikoes profoundly to the two young men, lifting up his hands in the deepest reverence of Burmah.

"The Lord of the Earth and the Sky desires his sons; he nears the Great Unknown."

CURTAIN

SCENE IV

The retreat of hip loong, the Wizard.

Time: the same night.

The curtain discovers mah phru, who has returned to human form, and the Wizard together.

He tells her that he has restored her to her former state only because she has implored him to do so; that her life is measured by hours as a consequence of such insensate folly in breaking the vow of five years back.

"But the King will live," she murmurs.

"The King will live. He will find happiness with someone fairer than you. That is well. Your life for his. It is the price."

"The price is nothing. Have I not looked on my heart's beloved one for five years—looked on his face—heard his voice—trembled with joy at his footsteps? Have I not waited and watched? Have I not gazed on my sons and seen their royal bearing, and known their touch?"

"You are, then, content?"

"You are a Wizard—you can read that I am."

"It is not I that am a Wizard—it is Love. That is the only Wizard this world knows."

CURTAIN

SCENE V

The bed-chamber of the King—vast and shadowy. On heaped-up cushions and covers of yellow and blue, under a pearl-sewn creamy velvet baldaquin, embroidered with peacocks, lies meng beng, mortally stricken; his face bears the ashen pallor that only dark skins know. The ministers, the servants, the courtiers, the countless motley gathering of an Eastern Court are scattered in anxious groups, watching, waiting, murmuring. Only the space near the couch is clear. Without, the dawn breaks over the sea, and, stealing through the opening, makes the great chamber flush till it looks like porphyry.

The tolling of a deep gong and the voices of a myriad birds invade the throbbing silence of the Palace.

"He passes," murmur the physicians. Everyone's gaze turns to the dying man.

"Yet his star is in the ascendant," say the astrologers. The risen sun touches him with its light like a caress. He opens his eyes. His sons advance. They raise him high on his cushions and give a restorative. The end has come. Suddenly he rallies slightly.

The doors at the far end are rudely opened. A woman, young and lovely, advances, thrusting roughly aside the many hands stretched out to bar her path.

She reaches the King.

"I bring you life, Star of my Soul," she cries, "I bring you life," and so saying, falls dead at his feet.

165

The Courtiers rush forward.

The King rises.

He stands erect.

The sun lies like a golden benediction over all.

Jewels glitter.

The whole world of birds sing.

THE CURTAIN FALLS

Footnotes:

[4] One of the greatest feasts of the Buddhist year.

[6] Spire.

[32] Fairy.

IMPRESSIONS OF AMERICA

TO
WALTER LEDGER:
PIGNUS
AMICITIÆ.

IMPRESSIONS.

I.

LE JARDIN.

The lily's withered chalice falls
Around its rod of dusty gold,
And from the beech trees on the wold
The last wood-pigeon coos and calls.

The gaudy leonine sunflower
Hangs black and barren on its stalk,
And down the windy garden walk
The dead leaves scatter,—hour by hour.

Pale privet-petals white as milk
Are blown into a snowy mass;
The roses lie upon the grass,
Like little shreds of crimson silk.

II.

LA MER.

A white mist drifts across the shrouds,
A wild moon in this wintry sky
Gleams like an angry lion's eye
Out of a mane of tawny clouds.

The muffled steersman at the wheel

Is but a shadow in the gloom;—

And in the throbbing engine room

Leap the long rods of polished steel.

The shattered storm has left its trace

Upon this huge and heaving dome,

For the thin threads of yellow foam

Float on the waves like ravelled lace.

Oscar Wilde.

PREFACE.

Oscar Wilde visited America in the year 1882. Interest in the Æsthetic School, of which he was already the acknowledged master, had sometime previously spread to the United States, and it is said that the production of the Gilbert and Sullivan opera, "Patience,"[1] in which he and his disciples were held up to ridicule, determined him to pay a visit to the States to give some lectures explaining what he meant by Æstheticism, hoping thereby to interest, and possibly to instruct and elevate our transatlantic cousins.

He set sail on board the "Arizona" on Saturday, December 24th, 1881, arriving in New York early in the following year. On landing he was bombarded by journalists eager to interview the distinguished stranger. "Punch," in its issue of January 14th, in a happy vein, parodied these interviewers, the most amusing passage in which referred to "His Glorious Past," wherein Wilde was made to say, "Precisely—I took the Newdigate. Oh! no doubt, every year some man gets the Newdigate; but not every year does Newdigate get an Oscar."

At Omaha, where, under the auspices of the Social Art Club, Wilde delivered a lecture on "Decorative Art," he described his impressions of many American houses as being "illy designed, decorated shabbily, and in bad taste, filled with furniture that was not honestly made,   and was out of character." This statement gave rise to the following verses:—

What a shame and what a pity,

In the streets of London City

Mr. Wilde is seen no more.

Far from Piccadilly banished,

He to Omaha has vanished.

Horrid place, which swells ignore.

On his back a coat he beareth,

Such as Sir John Bennet weareth,

Made of velvet—strange array!

Legs Apollo might have sighed for,

Or great Hercules have died for,

His knee breeches now display.

Waving sunflower and lily,

He calls all the houses "illy

Decorated and designed."

For of taste they've not a tittle;

They may chew and they may whittle;

But they're all born colour-blind!

His lectures dealt almost exclusively with the subjects of Art and Dress Reform. In the course of one lecture he remarked that the most impressive room he had yet entered in America was the one in Camden Town where he met Walt Whitman. It contained plenty of fresh air and sunlight. On the table was a simple cruse of water. This led to a parody, in the style of Whitman, describing an imaginary interview between the two poets, which appeared in "The Century" a few months later. Wilde is called Narcissus and Whitman Paumanokides.

Paumanokides:—

Who may this be?

This young man clad unusually with loose locks, languorous, glidingly toward me advancing,

Toward the ceiling of my chamber his orbic and expressive eyeballs uprolling, and so on, to which Narcissus replies,

O clarion, from whose brazen throat,

Strange sounds across the seas are blown,

Where England, girt as with a moat,

A strong sea-lion sits alone!

Of the lectures which he delivered in America only one has been preserved, namely that on the English Renaissance. This was his first lecture, and it was delivered in New York on January 9th, 1882. According to a contemporary account in the "New York Herald" a distinguished and crowded audience assembled in Chickering Hall that evening to listen to one who "was well worth seeing, his short breeches and silk stockings showing to even better advantage upon the stage than in the gilded drawing-rooms, where the young Apostle has heretofore been seen in New York."[2]

On leaving the States in the "fall" of the year Wilde proceeded to Canada and thence to Nova Scotia, arriving in Halifax in the second week of October. Of his visit there we have no record except an amusing interview described in a local paper a few days later. He was dressed in a velvet jacket with an ordinary linen collar and neck tie and he wore trousers. "Mr. Wilde," the interviewer states, "was communicative and genial; he said he found Canada pleasant, but in answer to a question as to whether European or American women were the more beautiful, he dexterously evaded his querist."

As regards poetry he expressed his opinion that Poe was the greatest American poet, and that Walt Whitman, if not a poet, was a man who sounded a strong note, perhaps neither prose nor poetry, but something of his own that was "grand, original and unique."

During his tour in America Wilde "happened to find" himself (as he has himself described it), in Louisville, Kentucky. The subject he had selected to speak on was the Mission of Art in the Nineteenth Century. In the course of his lecture he had occasion to quote Keats' Sonnet on Blue "as an example of the poet's delicate sense of colour-harmonies." After the lecture there came round to see him "a lady of middle age, with a sweet gentle manner and most musical voice," who introduced herself as Mrs. Speed, the daughter of George Keats, and she invited the lecturer to come and examine the Keats manuscripts in her possession.

Some months afterwards when lecturing in California he received a letter from this lady asking him to accept the original manuscript of the sonnet which he had quoted.

Mention must be made of Wilde's first play, a drama in blank verse entitled "Vera, or the Nihilists." It had been arranged that, before his departure for America, this play should be performed at the Adelphi Theatre, London, with Mrs. Bernard Beere as the heroine, on Saturday, December 17th, 1881, but a few weeks before the date fixed for the first performance, the author decided to postpone the production "owing to the state of political feeling in England."

On his return to England in 1883 Wilde started on a lecturing tour, the first being to the Art Students of the Royal Academy at their Club in Golden Square on June 30th. Ten days later he spoke at Prince's Hall on his "Personal Impressions of America," and on subsequent occasions at Margate, Ramsgate and Southampton. On Monday, July 30th he lectured at Southport and on the following Thursday he went to Liverpool to welcome Mrs. Langtry on her return from America, and the same afternoon he left on his second visit to the States in order to superintend the rehearsals of "Vera," which it had been arranged to produce at the Union Square Theatre, New York, on August 20th following. The piece was not a success—it was, indeed, the only failure Wilde had. However, his next play, which he called his "Opus Secundum," also a blank verse tragedy, had a successful run in America in 1891. This was "The Duchess of Padua," played by Lawrence Barrett, under the title of "Guido Ferranti." This has not been seen in England, nor is it even possible for Wilde's admirers to read this early offspring of his pen, for only twenty copies were printed for acting purposes in America and of these but one is known to be in existence, in this country at least.

An authorised German translation was made by Max Meyerfeld and the first performance took place at the German Theatre in Hamburg about a year ago. An English version is advertised from a piratical publisher in Paris but it is only a translation from the German back into English.

Towards the end of September 1883 Oscar Wilde returned to England and immediately began "an all round lecturing tour," his first visit being to Wandsworth Town Hall on Monday, September 24th, when he delivered to an enthusiastic audience a lecture on his "Impressions of America," which is contained in the following pages. He was dressed, a London paper of the time states, "in ordinary evening costume, and carried an orange-coloured silk handkerchief in his breast. He spoke with great fluency, in a voice now and then singularly musical, and only once or twice made a scarcely perceptible reference to notes." The lecture was under the auspices of a local Literary Society, and the principle residents of the district turned out "en masse." The Chairman, the Rev. John Park, in introducing the lecturer, said there were two reasons why he was glad to welcome him, and he thought his own feelings would be shared by the audience. They must all plead guilty to a feeling of curiosity, he hoped a laudable one, to see and hear Mr. Wilde for his own sake, and they were also glad to hear about America—a country which many might regard as a kind of Elysium.

On March 5th in the following year Wilde lectured at the Crystal Palace on his American experiences, and on April 26th he "preached his Gospel in the East-end," when it is recorded that his audience was not only delighted with his humour, but was "surprised at the excellent good sense he talked." His subject was a plea in favour of "art for schools," and many of his remarks about the English system of elementary education—with its insistence on "the population of places that no one ever wants to go to," and its "familiarity with the lives of persons who probably never existed"—were said to be quite worthy of Ruskin. A contemporary account adds that Wilde "showed himself a pupil of Mr. Ruskin's, too, in insisting on the importance of every child being taught some handicraft, and in looking forward to the time when a boy would rather look at a bird or even draw it than throw "his customary stone!"

The British "gamin" has not made much progress in this respect during the last twenty years!

His lectures on "Dress," with the newspaper correspondence which they evoked, including some of Oscar Wilde's replies in his most characteristic vein, must be reserved for a future volume.

STUART MASON.

Oxford, January 1906.

1. First produced at the Opera Comique, April 23rd, 1881. Wilde was burlesqued as Reginald Bunthorne, a Fleshly Poet.

2. Wilde repeated this lecture throughout the States during his tour. At Rochester, on February 7th, he met with a most disorderly reception on the part of the College Students. Two days later Mr. Joaquin Miller, of St. Louis, wrote to Wilde saying that he had "read with shame about the behaviour of those ruffians." To this Wilde replied, "I thank you for your chivalrous and courteous letter," and in the course of his letter makes a more special attack on that critic whom he terms "the itinerant libeller of New England."

IMPRESSIONS OF AMERICA.

I fear I cannot picture America as altogether an Elysium—perhaps, from the ordinary standpoint I know but little about the country. I cannot give its latitude or longitude; I cannot compute the value of its dry goods, and I have no very close acquaintance with its politics. These are matters which may not interest you, and they certainly are not interesting to me.

The first thing that struck me on landing in America was that if the Americans are not the most well-dressed people in the world, they are the most comfortably dressed. Men are seen there with the dreadful chimney-pot hat, but there are very few hatless men; men wear the shocking swallow-tail coat, but few are to be seen with no coat at all. There is an air of comfort in the appearance of the people which is a marked contrast to that seen in this country, where, too often, people are seen in close contact with rags.

The next thing particularly noticeable is that everybody seems in a hurry to catch a train. This is a state of things which is not favourable to poetry or romance. Had Romeo or Juliet been in a constant state of anxiety about trains, or had their minds been agitated by the question of return-tickets, Shakespeare could not have given us those lovely balcony scenes which are so full of poetry and pathos.

America is the noisiest country that ever existed. One is waked up in the morning, not by the singing of the nightingale, but by the steam whistle. It is surprising that the sound practical sense of the Americans does not reduce this intolerable noise. All Art depends upon exquisite and delicate sensibility, and such continual turmoil must ultimately be destructive of the musical faculty.

There is not so much beauty to be found in American cities as in Oxford, Cambridge, Salisbury or Winchester, where are lovely relics of a beautiful age; but still there is a good deal of beauty to be seen in them now and then, but only where the American has not attempted to create it. Where the Americans have attempted to produce beauty they have signally failed. A remarkable characteristic of the Americans is the manner in which they have applied science to modern life.

This is apparent in the most cursory stroll through New York. In England an inventor is regarded almost as a   crazy man, and in too many instances invention ends in disappointment and poverty. In America an inventor is honoured, help is forthcoming, and the exercise of ingenuity, the application of science to the work of man, is there the shortest road to wealth. There is no country in the world where machinery is so lovely as in America.

I have always wished to believe that the line of strength and the line of beauty are one. That wish was realised when I contemplated American machinery. It was not until I had seen the water-works at Chicago that I realised the wonders of machinery; the rise and fall of the steel rods, the symmetrical motion of the great wheels is the most beautifully rhythmic thing I have ever seen.[3]   One is impressed in America, but not favourably impressed, by the inordinate size of everything. The country seems to try to bully one into a belief in its power by its impressive bigness.

I was disappointed with Niagara—most people must be disappointed with Niagara. Every American bride is taken there, and the sight of the stupendous waterfall must be one of the earliest, if not the keenest, disappointments in American married life. One sees it under bad conditions, very far away, the point of view not showing the splendour of the water. To appreciate it really one has to see it from underneath the fall, and to do that it is necessary to be dressed in a yellow oil-skin, which is as ugly as a mackintosh—and I hope none of you ever wears one. It is a consolation to know, however, that such an artist as Madame Bernhardt has not only worn that yellow, ugly dress, but has been photographed in it.

Perhaps the most beautiful part of America is the West, to reach which, however, involves a journey by rail of six days, racing along tied to an ugly tin-kettle of a steam engine. I found but poor consolation for this journey in the fact that the boys who infest the cars and sell everything that one can eat—or should not eat—were selling editions of my poems vilely printed on a kind of grey blotting paper, for the low price of ten cents.[4] Calling these boys on one side I told them that though poets like to be popular they desire to be paid, and selling editions of my poems without giving me a profit is dealing a blow at literature which must have a disastrous effect on poetical aspirants. The invariable reply that they made was that they themselves made a profit out of the transaction and that was all they cared about.

It is a popular superstition that in America a visitor is invariably addressed as "Stranger." I was never once addressed as "Stranger." When I went to Texas I was called "Captain"; when I got to the centre of the country I was addressed as "Colonel," and, on arriving at the borders of Mexico, as "General." On the whole, however, "Sir," the old English method of addressing people is the most common.

It is, perhaps, worth while to note that what many people call Americanisms are really old English expressions which have lingered in our colonies while they have been lost in our own country. Many people imagine that the term "I guess," which is so common in America, is purely an American expression, but it was used by John Locke in his work on "The Understanding," just as we now use "I think."[5]

It is in the colonies, and not in the mother country, that the old life of the country really exists. If one wants to realise what English Puritanism is— not at its worst (when it is very bad), but at its best, and then it is not very good—I do not think one can find much of it in England, but much can be found about Boston and Massachusetts. We have got rid of it. America still preserves it, to be, I hope, a short-lived curiosity.

San Francisco is a really beautiful city. China Town, peopled by Chinese labourers, is the most artistic town I have ever come across. The people— strange, melancholy Orientals, whom many people would call common, and they are certainly very poor—have determined that they will have nothing about them that is not beautiful. In the Chinese restaurant, where these navvies meet to have supper in the evening, I found them drinking tea out of china cups as delicate as the petals of a rose-leaf, whereas at the gaudy hotels I was supplied with a delf cup an inch and a half thick. When the Chinese bill was presented it was made out on rice paper, the account being done in Indian ink as fantastically as if an artist had been etching little birds on a fan.

Salt Lake City contains only two buildings of note, the chief being the Tabernacle, which is in the shape of a soup-kettle. It is decorated by the only native artist, and he has treated religious subjects in the naive spirit of the early Florentine painters, representing people of our own day in the dress of the period side by side with people of Biblical history who are clothed in some romantic costume.

The building next in importance is called the Amelia Palace, in honour of one of Brigham Young's wives. When he died the present president of the Mormons stood up in the Tabernacle and said that it had been revealed to him that he was to have the Amelia Palace, and that on this subject there were to be no more revelations of any kind!

From Salt Lake City one travels over the great plains of Colorado and up the Rocky Mountains, on the top of which is Leadville, the richest city in the world. It has also got the reputation of being the roughest, and every man carries a revolver. I was told that if I went there they would be sure to shoot me or my travelling manager. I wrote and told them that nothing that they could do to my travelling manager would intimidate me. They are miners—men working in metals, so I lectured to them on the Ethics of Art. I read them passages from the autobiography of Benvenuto Cellini and they seemed much delighted. I was reproved by my hearers for not having brought him with me. I explained that he had been dead for some little time which elicited the enquiry "Who shot him"? They afterwards took me to a dancing saloon where I saw the only rational method of art criticism I have ever come across. Over the piano was printed a notice:—

PLEASE DO NOT SHOOT THE PIANIST.

HE IS DOING HIS BEST.

The mortality among pianists in that place is marvellous. Then they asked me to supper, and having accepted, I had to descend a mine in a rickety bucket in which it was impossible to be graceful. Having got into the heart of the mountain I had supper, the first course being whisky, the second whisky and the third whisky.

I went to the Theatre to lecture and I was informed that just before I went there two men had been seized for committing a murder, and in that theatre they had been brought on to the stage at eight o'clock in the evening, and then and there tried and executed before a crowded audience. But I found these miners very charming and not at all rough.

Among the more elderly inhabitants of the South I found a melancholy tendency to date every event of importance by the late war. "How beautiful the moon is to-night," I once remarked to a gentleman who was standing next to me. "Yes," was his reply, "but you should have seen it before the war."

So infinitesimal did I find the knowledge of Art, west of the Rocky Mountains, that an art patron—one who in his day had been a miner—actually sued the railroad company for damages because the plaster cast of Venus of Milo, which he had imported from Paris, had been delivered minus the arms. And, what is more surprising still, he gained his case and the damages.

Pennsylvania, with its rocky gorges and woodland scenery, reminded me of Switzerland. The prairie reminded me of a piece of blotting-paper.

The Spanish and French have left behind them memorials in the beauty of their names. All the cities that have beautiful names derive them from the Spanish or the French. The English people give intensely ugly names to places. One place had such an ugly name that I refused to lecture there. It was called Grigsville. Supposing I had founded a school of Art there—fancy "Early Grigsville." Imagine a School of Art teaching "Grigsville Renaissance."

As for slang I did not hear much of it, though a young lady who had changed her clothes after an afternoon dance did say that "after the heel kick she shifted her day goods."

American youths are pale and precocious, or sallow and supercilious, but

American girls are pretty and charming—little oases of pretty unreasonableness in a vast desert of practical common-sense.

Every American girl is entitled to have twelve young men devoted to her. They remain her slaves and she rules them with charming nonchalance.

The men are entirely given to business; they have, as they say, their brains in front of their heads. They are also exceedingly acceptive of new ideas. Their education is practical. We base the education of children entirely on books, but we must give a child a mind before we can instruct the mind. Children have a natural antipathy to books—handicraft should be the basis of education. Boys and girls should be taught to use their hands to make something, and they would be less apt to destroy and be mischievous.

In going to America one learns that poverty is not a necessary accompaniment to civilisation. There at any rate is a country that has no trappings, no pageants and no gorgeous ceremonies. I saw only two processions—one was the Fire Brigade preceded by the Police, the other was the Police preceded by the Fire Brigade.

Every man when he gets to the age of twenty-one is allowed a vote, and thereby immediately acquires his political education. The Americans are the best politically educated people in the world. It is well worth one's while to go to a country which can teach us the beauty of the word FREEDOM and the value of the thing LIBERTY.

3. In a poem published in an American magazine on February 15th, 1882, Wilde wrote

"And in the throbbing engine room

Leap the long rods of polished steel."

4. Poems by Oscar Wilde. Also his Lecture on the English Renaissance. The Seaside Library, Vol. lviii. No. 1183, January 19th, 1882. 4to. Pp. 32. New York: George Munro, Publisher.

A copy of this edition was sold by auction in New York last year for eight dollars.

5. See An Essay concerning Human Understanding, IV. xii. 10.

A still more striking instance of the use of this expression is to be found in the same writer's Thoughts concerning Education, s. 28, where he says:— "Once in four and twenty hours, I think, is enough; and nobody, I guess, will think it too much."

OSCAR WILDE IN AMERICA.

An interesting account of Oscar Wilde, at the time of his American tour, was given in the Lady's Pictorial a few weeks after his arrival in New York, the city which he described as "one huge Whiteley's shop."

His Abode.

He was interviewed in a room which was intensely warm and the sofa on which the poet reclined was drawn up to the fire. An immense wolf rug, bordered with scarlet, was thrown over it and half-encircled his graceful form in its warm embrace. Wilde was wearied. In a languid, half enervated manner he gently sipped hot chocolate from a cup by his side. Occasionally he inhaled a long, deep whiff from a smouldering cigarette held lightly in his white and shapely hand.

His Dress.

He was attired in a smoking suit of dark brown velvet faced with lapels of red quilted silk. The ends of a long dark necktie floated over the facing like sea-weed on foam tinged by the dying sun. Dark brown nether garments, striped with red up the seam, and patent leather shoes with light cloth uppers completed the rest of the poet's costume.

His favourite colour is said to have been something between brown and green, a tint "that never was on sea or sky," and he had a complete suit made of it. A white walking-stick which he was in the habit of carrying was presented to him at the Acropolis and was said to have been cut from the olive groves of the Academia. Only in the evening was he wont to don knee breeches, "but evening and morning alike," adds his interviewer, "find him neither more nor less than a man, and always a perfect gentleman."

His appearance.

Long masses of dark brown hair, parted in the middle, fell in odd curves of beauty over his broad shoulders. He wore neither beard nor moustache.

The full, rather sensuous lips, now pressed close together with momentary tension, now parted in kindly smile, showed to perfection the nobility of his countenance.

A Grecian nose and a well-tinged flush of health on the poet's face added all that was required to make it a truly remarkable one. The eyes were large, dark[6] and ever-changing in expression. He was a charming companion who could tell racy stories and repeat bons mots of those whom society delighted to honour, and at the same time could cap quotations from Greek authors.

6. A French writer, M. Joseph-Renaud, recently described Wilde's eyes as being blue, while Lord Alfred Douglas affirms that they were green.

About Author

Oscar Fingal O'Flahertie Wills Wilde (16 October 1854 – 30 November 1900) was an Irish poet and playwright. After writing in different forms throughout the 1880s, the early 1890s saw him become one of the most popular playwrights in London. He is best remembered for his epigrams and plays, his novel The Picture of Dorian Gray, and the circumstances of his criminal conviction for "gross indecency", imprisonment, and early death at age 46.

Wilde's parents were successful Anglo-Irish intellectuals in Dublin. A young Wilde learned to speak fluent French and German. At university, Wilde read Greats; he demonstrated himself to be an exceptional classicist, first at Trinity College Dublin, then at Oxford. He became associated with the emerging philosophy of aestheticism, led by two of his tutors, Walter Pater and John Ruskin. After university, Wilde moved to London into fashionable cultural and social circles.

As a spokesman for aestheticism, he tried his hand at various literary activities: he published a book of poems, lectured in the United States and Canada on the new "English Renaissance in Art" and interior decoration, and then returned to London where he worked prolifically as a journalist. Known for his biting wit, flamboyant dress and glittering conversational skill, Wilde became one of the best-known personalities of his day. At the turn of the 1890s, he refined his ideas about the supremacy of art in a series of dialogues and essays, and incorporated themes of decadence, duplicity, and beauty into what would be his only novel, The Picture of Dorian Gray (1890). The opportunity to construct aesthetic details precisely, and combine them with larger social themes, drew Wilde to write drama. He wrote Salome (1891) in French while in Paris but it was refused a licence for England due to an absolute prohibition on the portrayal of Biblical subjects on the English stage. Unperturbed, Wilde produced four society comedies in the early 1890s, which made him one of the most successful playwrights of late-Victorian London.

At the height of his fame and success, while The Importance of Being Earnest (1895) was still being performed in London, Wilde had the Marquess of Queensberry prosecuted for criminal libel. The Marquess was the father of Wilde's lover, Lord Alfred Douglas. The libel trial unearthed evidence that caused Wilde to drop his charges and led to his own arrest and trial for gross indecency with men. After two more trials he was convicted and sentenced to two years' hard labour, the maximum penalty, and was jailed from 1895 to 1897. During his last year in prison, he wrote De Profundis (published posthumously in 1905), a long letter which discusses his spiritual journey through his trials, forming a dark counterpoint to his earlier philosophy of pleasure. On his release, he left immediately for France, never to return to Ireland or Britain. There he wrote his last work, The Ballad of Reading Gaol (1898), a long poem commemorating the harsh rhythms of prison life.

Early life

Oscar Wilde was born at 21 Westland Row, Dublin (now home of the Oscar Wilde Centre, Trinity College), the second of three children born to Anglo-Irish Sir William Wilde and Jane Wilde, two years behind his brother William ("Willie"). Wilde's mother had distant Italian ancestry, and under the pseudonym "Speranza" (the Italian word for 'hope'), wrote poetry for the revolutionary Young Irelanders in 1848; she was a lifelong Irish nationalist. She read the Young Irelanders' poetry to Oscar and Willie, inculcating a love of these poets in her sons. Lady Wilde's interest in the neo-classical revival showed in the paintings and busts of ancient Greece and Rome in her home.

William Wilde was Ireland's leading oto-ophthalmologic (ear and eye) surgeon and was knighted in 1864 for his services as medical adviser and assistant commissioner to the censuses of Ireland. He also wrote books about Irish archaeology and peasant folklore. A renowned philanthropist, his dispensary for the care of the city's poor at the rear of Trinity College, Dublin, was the forerunner of the Dublin Eye and Ear Hospital, now located at Adelaide Road. On his father's side Wilde was descended from a Dutchman, Colonel de Wilde, who went to Ireland with King William of Orange's invading army in 1690, and numerous Anglo-Irish ancestors. On his mother's side, Wilde's ancestors included a bricklayer from County Durham, who emigrated to Ireland sometime in the 1770s.

Wilde was baptised as an infant in St. Mark's Church, Dublin, the local Church of Ireland (Anglican) church. When the church was closed, the records were moved to the nearby St. Ann's Church, Dawson Street. Davis Coakley mentions a second baptism by a Catholic priest, Father Prideaux Fox, who befriended Oscar's mother circa 1859. According to Fox's testimony in Donahoe's Magazine in 1905, Jane Wilde would visit his chapel in Glencree, County Wicklow, for Mass and would take her sons with her. She asked Father Fox in this period to baptise her sons.

Fox described it in this way:

"I am not sure if she ever became a Catholic herself but it was not long before she asked me to instruct two of her children, one of them being the future erratic genius, Oscar Wilde. After a few weeks I baptized these two children, Lady Wilde herself being present on the occasion.

In addition to his children with his wife, Sir William Wilde was the father of three children born out of wedlock before his marriage: Henry Wilson, born in 1838 to one woman, and Emily and Mary Wilde, born in 1847 and 1849, respectively, to a second woman. Sir William acknowledged paternity of his illegitimate or "natural" children and provided for their education, arranging for them to be reared by his relatives rather than with his legitimate children in his family household with his wife.

In 1855, the family moved to No. 1 Merrion Square, where Wilde's sister, Isola, was born in 1857. The Wildes' new home was larger. With both his parents' success and delight in social life, the house soon became the site of a "unique medical and cultural milieu". Guests at their salon included Sheridan Le Fanu, Charles Lever, George Petrie, Isaac Butt, William Rowan Hamilton and Samuel Ferguson.

Until he was nine, Oscar Wilde was educated at home, where a French nursemaid and a German governess taught him their languages. He attended Portora Royal School in Enniskillen, County Fermanagh, from 1864 to 1871. Until his early twenties, Wilde summered at the villa, Moytura House, which his father had built in Cong, County Mayo. There the young Wilde and his brother Willie played with George Moore.

Isola died at age nine of meningitis. Wilde's poem "Requiescat" is written to her memory.

> "Tread lightly, she is near
>
> Under the snow
>
> Speak gently, she can hear
>
> the daisies grow"

University education: 1870s

Trinity College, Dublin

Wilde left Portora with a royal scholarship to read classics at Trinity College, Dublin, from 1871 to 1874, sharing rooms with his older brother Willie Wilde. Trinity, one of the leading classical schools, placed him with scholars such as R. Y. Tyrell, Arthur Palmer, Edward Dowden and his tutor, Professor J. P. Mahaffy, who inspired his interest in Greek literature. As a student Wilde worked with Mahaffy on the latter's book Social Life in Greece. Wilde, despite later reservations, called Mahaffy "my first and best teacher" and "the scholar who showed me how to love Greek things".For his part, Mahaffy boasted of having created Wilde; later, he said Wilde was "the only blot on my tutorship".

The University Philosophical Society also provided an education, as members discussed intellectual and artistic subjects such as Dante Gabriel Rossetti and Algernon Charles Swinburne weekly. Wilde quickly became an established member – the members' suggestion book for 1874 contains two pages of banter (sportingly) mocking Wilde's emergent aestheticism. He presented a paper titled "Aesthetic Morality". At Trinity, Wilde established himself as an outstanding student: he came first in his class in his first year, won a scholarship by competitive examination in his second and, in his finals, won the Berkeley Gold Medal in Greek, the University's highest academic award. He was encouraged to compete for a demyship to Magdalen College, Oxford – which he won easily, having already studied Greek for over nine years.

Magdalen College, Oxford

At Magdalen, he read Greats from 1874 to 1878, and from there he applied to join the Oxford Union, but failed to be elected.

Attracted by its dress, secrecy, and ritual, Wilde petitioned the Apollo Masonic Lodge at Oxford, and was soon raised to the "Sublime Degree of Master Mason".During a resurgent interest in Freemasonry in his third year, he commented he "would be awfully sorry to give it up if I secede from the Protestant Heresy". Wilde's active involvement in Freemasonry lasted only for the time he spent at Oxford; he allowed his membership of the Apollo University Lodge to lapse after failing to pay subscriptions.

Catholicism deeply appealed to him, especially its rich liturgy, and he discussed converting to it with clergy several times. In 1877, Wilde was left speechless after an audience with Pope Pius IX in Rome.He eagerly read the books of Cardinal Newman, a noted Anglican priest who had converted to Catholicism and risen in the church hierarchy. He became more serious in 1878, when he met the Reverend Sebastian Bowden, a priest in the Brompton Oratory who had received some high-profile converts. Neither his father, who threatened to cut off his funds, nor Mahaffy thought much of the plan; but mostly Wilde, the supreme individualist, balked at the last minute from pledging himself to any formal creed. On the appointed day of his baptism, Wilde sent Father Bowden a bunch of altar lilies instead. Wilde did retain a lifelong interest in Catholic theology and liturgy.

While at Magdalen College, Wilde became particularly well known for his role in the aesthetic and decadent movements. He wore his hair long, openly scorned "manly" sports though he occasionally boxed, and he decorated his rooms with peacock feathers, lilies, sunflowers, blue china and other objets d'art. He once remarked to friends, whom he entertained lavishly, "I find it harder and harder every day to live up to my blue china." The line quickly became famous, accepted as a slogan by aesthetes but used against them by critics who sensed in it a terrible vacuousness. Some elements disdained the aesthetes, but their languishing attitudes and showy costumes became a recognised pose. Wilde was once physically attacked by a group of four fellow students, and dealt with them single-handedly, surprising critics. By his third year Wilde had truly begun to develop himself and his myth, and considered his learning to be more expansive than what was within the prescribed texts. This attitude resulted in his being rusticated for one term, after he had returned late to a college term from a trip to Greece with Mahaffy.

Wilde did not meet Walter Pater until his third year, but had been enthralled by his Studies in the History of the Renaissance, published during Wilde's final year in Trinity. Pater argued that man's sensibility to beauty should be refined above all else, and that each moment should be felt to its fullest extent. Years later, in De Profundis, Wilde described Pater's Studies... as "that book that has had such a strange influence over my life".He learned tracts of the book by heart, and carried it with him on travels in later years. Pater gave Wilde his sense of almost flippant devotion to art, though he gained a purpose for it through the lectures and writings of critic John Ruskin. Ruskin despaired at the self-validating aestheticism of Pater, arguing that the importance of art lies in its potential for the betterment of society. Ruskin admired beauty, but believed it must be allied with, and applied to, moral good. When Wilde eagerly attended Ruskin's lecture series The Aesthetic and Mathematic Schools of Art in Florence, he learned about aesthetics as the non-mathematical elements of painting. Despite being given to neither early rising nor manual labour, Wilde volunteered for Ruskin's project to convert a swampy country lane into a smart road neatly edged with flowers.

Wilde won the 1878 Newdigate Prize for his poem "Ravenna", which reflected on his visit there the year before, and he duly read it at Encaenia. In November 1878, he graduated with a double first in his B.A. of Classical Moderations and Literae Humaniores (Greats). Wilde wrote to a friend, "The dons are 'astonied' beyond words – the Bad Boy doing so well in the end!"

Apprenticeship of an aesthete: 1880s

Debut in society

After graduation from Oxford, Wilde returned to Dublin, where he met again Florence Balcombe, a childhood sweetheart. She became engaged to Bram Stoker and they married in 1878. Wilde was disappointed but stoic:

196

he wrote to her, remembering "the two sweet years – the sweetest years of all my youth" during which they had been close. He also stated his intention to "return to England, probably for good." This he did in 1878, only briefly visiting Ireland twice after that.

Unsure of his next step, Wilde wrote to various acquaintances enquiring about Classics positions at Oxford or Cambridge. The Rise of Historical Criticism was his submission for the Chancellor's Essay prize of 1879, which, though no longer a student, he was still eligible to enter. Its subject, "Historical Criticism among the Ancients" seemed ready-made for Wilde – with both his skill in composition and ancient learning – but he struggled to find his voice with the long, flat, scholarly style. Unusually, no prize was awarded that year.

With the last of his inheritance from the sale of his father's houses, he set himself up as a bachelor in London. The 1881 British Census listed Wilde as a boarder at 1 (now 44) Tite Street, Chelsea, where Frank Miles, a society painter, was the head of the household. Wilde spent the next six years in London and Paris, and in the United States, where he travelled to deliver lectures.

He had been publishing lyrics and poems in magazines since entering Trinity College, especially in Kottabos and the Dublin University Magazine. In mid-1881, at 27 years old, he published Poems, which collected, revised and expanded his poems.

The book was generally well received, and sold out its first print run of 750 copies. Punch was less enthusiastic, saying "The poet is Wilde, but his poetry's tame". By a tight vote, the Oxford Union condemned the book for alleged plagiarism. The librarian, who had requested the book for the library, returned the presentation copy to Wilde with a note of apology.Biographer Richard Ellmann argues that Wilde's poem "Hélas!" was a sincere, though flamboyant, attempt to explain the dichotomies the poet saw in himself; one line reads: "To drift with every passion till my soul

Is a stringed lute on which all winds can play".

The book had further printings in 1882. It was bound in a rich, enamel parchment cover (embossed with gilt blossom) and printed on hand-made Dutch paper; over the next few years, Wilde presented many copies to the dignitaries and writers who received him during his lecture tours.

America: 1882

Aestheticism was sufficiently in vogue to be caricatured by Gilbert and Sullivan in Patience (1881). Richard D'Oyly Carte, an English impresario, invited Wilde to make a lecture tour of North America, simultaneously priming the pump for the US tour of Patience and selling this most charming aesthete to the American public. Wilde journeyed on the SS Arizona, arriving 2 January 1882, and disembarking the following day. Originally planned to last four months, it continued for almost a year due to the commercial success. Wilde sought to transpose the beauty he saw in art into daily life. This was a practical as well as philosophical project: in Oxford he had surrounded himself with blue china and lilies, and now one of his lectures was on interior design.

When asked to explain reports that he had paraded down Piccadilly in London carrying a lily, long hair flowing, Wilde replied, "It's not whether I did it or not that's important, but whether people believed I did it". Wilde believed that the artist should hold forth higher ideals, and that pleasure and beauty would replace utilitarian ethics.

Wilde and aestheticism were both mercilessly caricatured and criticised in the press; the Springfield Republican, for instance, commented on Wilde's behaviour during his visit to Boston to lecture on aestheticism, suggesting that Wilde's conduct was more a bid for notoriety rather than devotion to beauty and the aesthetic. T. W. Higginson, a cleric and abolitionist, wrote in "Unmanly Manhood" of his general concern that Wilde, "whose only distinction is that he has written a thin volume of very mediocre verse", would improperly influence the behaviour of men and women.

According to biographer Michèle Mendelssohn, Wilde was the subject of anti-Irish caricature and was portrayed as a monkey, a blackface performer and a Christy's Minstrel throughout his career. "Harper's Weekly put a sunflower-worshipping monkey dressed as Wilde on the front of the January 1882 issue. The magazine didn't let its reputation for quality impede its expression of what are now considered odious ethnic and racial ideologies. The drawing stimulated other American maligners and, in England, had a full-page reprint in the Lady's Pictorial. ... When the National Republican discussed Wilde, it was to explain 'a few items as to the animal's pedigree.' And on 22 January 1882 the Washington Post illustrated the Wild Man of Borneo alongside Oscar Wilde of England and asked 'How far is it from this to this?' "Though his press reception was hostile, Wilde was well received in diverse settings across America; he drank whiskey with miners in Leadville, Colorado, and was fêted at the most fashionable salons in many cities he visited.

London life and marriage

His earnings, plus expected income from The Duchess of Padua, allowed him to move to Paris between February and mid-May 1883. While there he met Robert Sherard, whom he entertained constantly. "We are dining on the Duchess tonight", Wilde would declare before taking him to an expensive restaurant. In August he briefly returned to New York for the production of Vera, his first play, after it was turned down in London. He reportedly entertained the other passengers with "Ave Imperatrix!, A Poem on England", about the rise and fall of empires. E. C. Stedman, in Victorian Poets, describes this "lyric to England" as "manly verse – a poetic and eloquent invocation". The play was initially well received by the audience, but when the critics wrote lukewarm reviews, attendance fell sharply and the play closed a week after it had opened.

Wilde had to return to England, where he continued to lecture on topics including Personal Impressions of America, The Value of Art in Modern Life, and Dress.

In London, he had been introduced in 1881 to Constance Lloyd, daughter of Horace Lloyd, a wealthy Queen's Counsel, and his wife. She happened to be visiting Dublin in 1884, when Wilde was lecturing at the Gaiety Theatre. He proposed to her, and they married on 29 May 1884 at the Anglican St James's Church, Paddington, in London. Although Constance had an annual allowance of £250, which was generous for a young woman (equivalent to about £25,600 in current value), the Wildes had relatively luxurious tastes. They had preached to others for so long on the subject of design that people expected their home to set new standards. No. 16, Tite Street was duly renovated in seven months at considerable expense. The couple had two sons together, Cyril (1885) and Vyvyan (1886). Wilde became the sole literary signatory of George Bernard Shaw's petition for a pardon of the anarchists arrested (and later executed) after the Haymarket massacre in Chicago in 1886.

Robert Ross had read Wilde's poems before they met at Oxford in 1886. He seemed unrestrained by the Victorian prohibition against homosexuality, and became estranged from his family. By Richard Ellmann's account, he was a precocious seventeen-year-old who "so young and yet so knowing, was determined to seduce Wilde". According to Daniel Mendelsohn, Wilde, who had long alluded to Greek love, was "initiated into homosexual sex" by Ross, while his "marriage had begun to unravel after his wife's second pregnancy, which left him physically repelled".

Prose writing: 1886–91

Journalism and editorship: 1886–89

Criticism over artistic matters in The Pall Mall Gazette provoked a letter in self-defence, and soon Wilde was a contributor to that and other journals during 1885–87. He enjoyed reviewing and journalism; the form suited his style. He could organise and share his views on art, literature and life, yet in a format less tedious than lecturing. Buoyed up, his reviews were largely chatty and positive. Wilde, like his parents before him, also supported the cause of Irish nationalism. When Charles Stewart Parnell was falsely accused of inciting murder, Wilde wrote a series of astute columns defending him in the Daily Chronicle.

His flair, having previously been put mainly into socialising, suited journalism and rapidly attracted notice. With his youth nearly over, and a family to support, in mid-1887 Wilde became the editor of The Lady's World magazine, his name prominently appearing on the cover. He promptly renamed it as The Woman's World and raised its tone, adding serious articles on parenting, culture, and politics, while keeping discussions of fashion and arts. Two pieces of fiction were usually included, one to be read to children, the other for the ladies themselves. Wilde worked hard to solicit good contributions from his wide artistic acquaintance, including those of Lady Wilde and his wife Constance, while his own "Literary and Other Notes" were themselves popular and amusing.

The initial vigour and excitement which he brought to the job began to fade as administration, commuting and office life became tedious. At the same time as Wilde's interest flagged, the publishers became concerned anew about circulation: sales, at the relatively high price of one shilling, remained low. Increasingly sending instructions to the magazine by letter, Wilde began a new period of creative work and his own column appeared less regularly.In October 1889, Wilde had finally found his voice in prose and, at the end of the second volume, Wilde left The Woman's World. The magazine outlasted him by one issue.

If Wilde's period at the helm of the magazine was a mixed success from an organizational point of view, it played a pivotal role in his development as a writer and facilitated his ascent to fame. Whilst Wilde the journalist supplied articles under the guidance of his editors, Wilde the editor was forced to learn to manipulate the literary marketplace on his own terms.

During the late 1880s, Wilde was a close friend of the artist James NcNeill Whistler and they dined together on many occasions. At one of these dinners, Whistler said a bon mot that Wilde found particularly witty, Wilde exclaimed that he wished that he had said it, and Whistler retorted "You will, Oscar, you will".Herbert Vivian—a mutual friend of Wilde and Whistler—attended the dinner and recorded it in his article The Reminiscences of a Short Life which appeared in The Sun in 1889. The article alleged that Wilde had a habit of passing off other people's witticisms as his own—especially Whistler's. Wilde considered Vivian's article to be a scurrilous betrayal, and it directly caused the broken friendship between Wilde and Whistler. The Reminiscences also caused great acrimony between Wilde and Vivian, Wilde accusing Vivian of "the inaccuracy of an eavesdropper with the method of a blackmailer" and banishing Vivian from his circle.

Shorter fiction

Wilde published The Happy Prince and Other Tales in 1888, and had been regularly writing fairy stories for magazines. In 1891 he published two more collections, Lord Arthur Savile's Crime and Other Stories, and in September A House of Pomegranates was dedicated "To Constance Mary Wilde". "The Portrait of Mr. W. H.", which Wilde had begun in 1887, was first published in Blackwood's Edinburgh Magazine in July 1889.It is a short story, which reports a conversation, in which the theory that Shakespeare's sonnets were written out of the poet's love of the boy actor "Willie Hughes", is advanced, retracted, and then propounded again. The only evidence for this is two supposed puns within the sonnets themselves.

The anonymous narrator is at first sceptical, then believing, finally flirtatious with the reader: he concludes that "there is really a great deal to be said of the Willie Hughes theory of Shakespeare's sonnets." By the end fact and fiction have melded together.Arthur Ransome wrote that Wilde "read something of himself into Shakespeare's sonnets" and became fascinated with the "Willie Hughes theory" despite the lack of biographical evidence for the historical William Hughes' existence. Instead of writing a short but serious essay on the question, Wilde tossed the theory amongst the three characters of the story, allowing it to unfold as background to the plot. The story thus is an early masterpiece of Wilde's combining many elements that interested him: conversation, literature and the idea that to shed oneself of an idea one must first convince another of its truth.Ransome concludes that Wilde succeeds precisely because the literary criticism is unveiled with such a deft touch.

Though containing nothing but "special pleading", it would not, he says "be possible to build an airier castle in Spain than this of the imaginary William Hughes" we continue listening nonetheless to be charmed by the telling. "You must believe in Willie Hughes," Wilde told an acquaintance, "I almost do, myself."

Essays and dialogues

Wilde, having tired of journalism, had been busy setting out his aesthetic ideas more fully in a series of longer prose pieces which were published in the major literary-intellectual journals of the day. In January 1889, The Decay of Lying: A Dialogue appeared in The Nineteenth Century, and Pen, Pencil and Poison, a satirical biography of Thomas Griffiths Wainewright, in The Fortnightly Review, edited by Wilde's friend Frank Harris. Two of Wilde's four writings on aesthetics are dialogues: though Wilde had evolved professionally from lecturer to writer, he retained an oral tradition of sorts. Having always excelled as a wit and raconteur, he often composed by assembling phrases, bons mots and witticisms into a longer, cohesive work.

Wilde was concerned about the effect of moralising on art; he believed in art's redemptive, developmental powers: "Art is individualism, and individualism is a disturbing and disintegrating force. There lies its immense value. For what it seeks is to disturb monotony of type, slavery of custom, tyranny of habit, and the reduction of man to the level of a machine." In his only political text, The Soul of Man Under Socialism, he argued political conditions should establish this primacy – private property should be abolished, and cooperation should be substituted for competition. At the same time, he stressed that the government most amenable to artists was no government at all. Wilde envisioned a society where mechanisation has freed human effort from the burden of necessity, effort which can instead be expended on artistic creation. George Orwell summarised, "In effect, the world will be populated by artists, each striving after perfection in the way that seems best to him."

This point of view did not align him with the Fabians, intellectual socialists who advocated using state apparatus to change social conditions, nor did it endear him to the monied classes whom he had previously entertained. Hesketh Pearson, introducing a collection of Wilde's essays in 1950, remarked how The Soul of Man Under Socialism had been an inspirational text for revolutionaries in Tsarist Russia but laments that in the Stalinist era "it is doubtful whether there are any uninspected places in which it could now be hidden".

Wilde considered including this pamphlet and The Portrait of Mr. W.H., his essay-story on Shakespeare's sonnets, in a new anthology in 1891, but eventually decided to limit it to purely aesthetic subjects. Intentions packaged revisions of four essays: The Decay of Lying, Pen, Pencil and Poison, The Truth of Masks (first published 1885), and The Critic as Artist in two parts. For Pearson the biographer, the essays and dialogues exhibit every aspect of Wilde's genius and character: wit, romancer, talker, lecturer, humanist and scholar and concludes that "no other productions of his have as varied an appeal". 1891 turned out to be Wilde's annus mirabilis; apart from his three collections he also produced his only novel.

The Picture of Dorian Gray

The first version of The Picture of Dorian Gray was published as the lead story in the July 1890 edition of Lippincott's Monthly Magazine, along with five others. The story begins with a man painting a picture of Gray. When Gray, who has a "face like ivory and rose leaves", sees his finished portrait, he breaks down. Distraught that his beauty will fade while the portrait stays beautiful, he inadvertently makes a Faustian bargain in which only the painted image grows old while he stays beautiful and young. For Wilde, the purpose of art would be to guide life as if beauty alone were its object. As Gray's portrait allows him to escape the corporeal ravages of his hedonism, Wilde sought to juxtapose the beauty he saw in art with daily life.

Reviewers immediately criticised the novel's decadence and homosexual allusions; The Daily Chronicle for example, called it "unclean", "poisonous", and "heavy with the mephitic odours of moral and spiritual putrefaction". Which he clarified his stance on ethics and aesthetics in art – "If a work of art is rich and vital and complete, those who have artistic instincts will see its beauty and those to whom ethics appeal more strongly will see its moral lesson." He nevertheless revised it extensively for book publication in 1891: six new chapters were added, some overtly decadent passages and homo-eroticism excised, and a preface was included consisting of twenty two epigrams, such as "Books are well written, or badly written. That is all."

Contemporary reviewers and modern critics have postulated numerous possible sources of the story, a search Jershua McCormack argues is futile because Wilde "has tapped a root of Western folklore so deep and ubiquitous that the story has escaped its origins and returned to the oral tradition." Wilde claimed the plot was "an idea that is as old as the history of literature but to which I have given a new form".Modern critic Robin McKie considered the novel to be technically mediocre, saying that the conceit of the plot had guaranteed its fame, but the device is never pushed to its full.On the other hand, Robert McCrum of The Guardian deemed it the 27th best novel ever written in English, calling it "an arresting, and slightly camp, exercise in late-Victorian gothic."

Theatrical career: 1892–95

Salomé

The 1891 census records the Wildes' residence at 16 Tite Street, where he lived with his wife Constance and two sons. Wilde though, not content with being better known than ever in London, returned to Paris in October 1891, this time as a respected writer. He was received at the salons littéraires, including the famous mardis of Stéphane Mallarmé, a renowned symbolist poet of the time. Wilde's two plays during the 1880s, Vera; or, The Nihilists and The Duchess of Padua, had not met with much success. He had continued his interest in the theatre and now, after finding his voice in prose, his thoughts turned again to the dramatic form as the biblical iconography of Salome filled his mind. One evening, after discussing depictions of Salome throughout history, he returned to his hotel and noticed a blank copybook lying on the desk, and it occurred to him to write in it what he had been saying. The result was a new play, Salomé, written rapidly and in French.

A tragedy, it tells the story of Salome, the stepdaughter of the tetrarch Herod Antipas, who, to her stepfather's dismay but mother's delight, requests the head of Jokanaan (John the Baptist) on a silver platter as a reward for dancing the Dance of the Seven Veils. When Wilde returned to London just before Christmas the Paris Echo referred to him as "le great event" of the season. Rehearsals of the play, starring Sarah Bernhardt, began but the play was refused a licence by the Lord Chamberlain, since it depicted biblical characters. Salome was published jointly in Paris and London in 1893, but was not performed until 1896 in Paris, during Wilde's later incarceration.

Comedies of society

Wilde, who had first set out to irritate Victorian society with his dress and talking points, then outrage it with Dorian Gray, his novel of vice hidden beneath art, finally found a way to critique society on its own terms. Lady Windermere's Fan was first performed on 20 February 1892 at St James's Theatre, packed with the cream of society. On the surface a witty comedy, there is subtle subversion underneath: "it concludes with collusive concealment rather than collective disclosure". The audience, like Lady Windermere, are forced to soften harsh social codes in favour of a more nuanced view. The play was enormously popular, touring the country for months, but largely trashed by conservative critics. It was followed by A Woman of No Importance in 1893, another Victorian comedy, revolving around the spectre of illegitimate births, mistaken identities and late revelations. Wilde was commissioned to write two more plays and An Ideal Husband, written in 1894, followed in January 1895.

Peter Raby said these essentially English plays were well-pitched, "Wilde, with one eye on the dramatic genius of Ibsen, and the other on the commercial competition in London's West End, targeted his audience with adroit precision".

Queensberry family

In mid-1891 Lionel Johnson introduced Wilde to Lord Alfred Douglas, Johnson's cousin and an undergraduate at Oxford at the time. Known to his family and friends as "Bosie", he was a handsome and spoilt young man. An intimate friendship sprang up between Wilde and Douglas and by 1893 Wilde was infatuated with Douglas and they consorted together regularly in a tempestuous affair. If Wilde was relatively indiscreet, even flamboyant, in the way he acted, Douglas was reckless in public. Wilde, who was earning up to £100 a week from his plays (his salary at The Woman's World had been £6), indulged Douglas's every whim: material, artistic or sexual.

Douglas soon initiated Wilde into the Victorian underground of gay prostitution and Wilde was introduced to a series of young working-class male prostitutes from 1892 onwards by Alfred Taylor. These infrequent rendezvous usually took the same form: Wilde would meet the boy, offer him gifts, dine him privately and then take him to a hotel room. Unlike Wilde's idealised relations with Ross, John Gray, and Douglas, all of whom remained part of his aesthetic circle, these consorts were uneducated and knew nothing of literature. Soon his public and private lives had become sharply divided; in De Profundis he wrote to Douglas that "It was like feasting with panthers; the danger was half the excitement... I did not know that when they were to strike at me it was to be at another's piping and at another's pay."

Douglas and some Oxford friends founded a journal, The Chameleon, to which Wilde "sent a page of paradoxes originally destined for the Saturday Review". "Phrases and Philosophies for the Use of the Young" was to come under attack six months later at Wilde's trial, where he was forced to defend the magazine to which he had sent his work.In any case, it became unique: The Chameleon was not published again.

Lord Alfred's father, the Marquess of Queensberry, was known for his outspoken atheism, brutish manner and creation of the modern rules of boxing. Queensberry, who feuded regularly with his son, confronted Wilde and Lord Alfred about the nature of their relationship several times, but Wilde was able to mollify him. In June 1894, he called on Wilde at 16 Tite Street, without an appointment, and clarified his stance: "I do not say that you are it, but you look it, and pose at it, which is just as bad. And if I catch you and my son again in any public restaurant I will thrash you" to which Wilde responded: "I don't know what the Queensberry rules are, but the Oscar Wilde rule is to shoot on sight".His account in De Profundis was less triumphant: "It was when, in my library at Tite Street, waving his small hands in the air in epileptic fury, your father... stood uttering every foul word his foul mind could think of, and screaming the loathsome threats he afterwards with such cunning carried out". Queensberry only described the scene once, saying Wilde had "shown him the white feather", meaning he had acted in a cowardly way. Though trying to remain calm, Wilde saw that he was becoming ensnared in a brutal family quarrel. He did not wish to bear Queensberry's insults, but he knew to confront him could lead to disaster were his liaisons disclosed publicly.

The Importance of Being Earnest

Wilde's final play again returns to the theme of switched identities: the play's two protagonists engage in "bunburying" (the maintenance of alternative personas in the town and country) which allows them to escape Victorian social mores.Earnest is even lighter in tone than Wilde's earlier comedies. While their characters often rise to serious themes in moments of crisis, Earnest lacks the by-now stock Wildean characters: there is no "woman with a past", the principals are neither villainous nor cunning, simply idle cultivés, and the idealistic young women are not that innocent. Mostly set in drawing rooms and almost completely lacking in action or violence, Earnest lacks the self-conscious decadence found in The Picture of Dorian Gray and Salome.

The play, now considered Wilde's masterpiece, was rapidly written in Wilde's artistic maturity in late 1894. It was first performed on 14 February 1895, at St James's Theatre in London, Wilde's second collaboration with George Alexander, the actor-manager. Both author and producer assiduously revised, prepared and rehearsed every line, scene and setting in the months before the premiere, creating a carefully constructed representation of late-Victorian society, yet simultaneously mocking it. During rehearsal Alexander requested that Wilde shorten the play from four acts to three, which the author did. Premieres at St James's seemed like "brilliant parties", and the opening of The Importance of Being Earnest was no exception. Allan Aynesworth (who played Algernon) recalled to Hesketh Pearson, "In my fifty-three years of acting, I never remember a greater triumph than [that] first night."Earnest's immediate reception as Wilde's best work to date finally crystallised his fame into a solid artistic reputation. The Importance of Being Earnest remains his most popular play.

Wilde's professional success was mirrored by an escalation in his feud with Queensberry. Queensberry had planned to insult Wilde publicly by throwing a bouquet of rotting vegetables onto the stage; Wilde was tipped off and had Queensberry barred from entering the theatre.Fifteen weeks later Wilde was in prison.

Trials

Wilde v. Queensberry

On 18 February 1895, the Marquess left his calling card at Wilde's club, the Albemarle, inscribed: "For Oscar Wilde, posing somdomite" Wilde, encouraged by Douglas and against the advice of his friends, initiated a private prosecution against Queensberry for libel, since the note amounted to a public accusation that Wilde had committed the crime of sodomy.

Queensberry was arrested for criminal libel; a charge carrying a possible sentence of up to two years in prison. Under the 1843 Libel Act, Queensberry could avoid conviction for libel only by demonstrating that his accusation was in fact true, and furthermore that there was some "public benefit" to having made the accusation openly. Queensberry's lawyers thus hired private detectives to find evidence of Wilde's homosexual liaisons.

Wilde's friends had advised him against the prosecution at a Saturday Review meeting at the Café Royal on 24 March 1895; Frank Harris warned him that "they are going to prove sodomy against you" and advised him to flee to France. Wilde and Douglas walked out in a huff, Wilde saying "it is at such moments as these that one sees who are one's true friends". The scene was witnessed by George Bernard Shaw who recalled it to Arthur Ransome a day or so before Ransome's trial for libelling Douglas in 1913. To Ransome it confirmed what he had said in his 1912 book on Wilde; that Douglas's rivalry for Wilde with Robbie Ross and his arguments with his father had resulted in Wilde's public disaster; as Wilde wrote in De Profundis. Douglas lost his case. Shaw included an account of the argument between Harris, Douglas and Wilde in the preface to his play The Dark Lady of the Sonnets.

The libel trial became a cause célèbre as salacious details of Wilde's private life with Taylor and Douglas began to appear in the press. A team of private detectives had directed Queensberry's lawyers, led by Edward Carson QC, to the world of the Victorian underground. Wilde's association with blackmailers and male prostitutes, cross-dressers and homosexual brothels was recorded, and various persons involved were interviewed, some being coerced to appear as witnesses since they too were accomplices to the crimes of which Wilde was accused.

The trial opened on 3 April 1895 before Justice Richard Henn Collins amid scenes of near hysteria both in the press and the public galleries. The extent of the evidence massed against Wilde forced him to declare meekly, "I am the prosecutor in this case"Wilde's lawyer, Sir Edward George Clarke, opened the case by pre-emptively asking Wilde about two suggestive letters Wilde had written to Douglas, which the defence had in its possession. He characterised the first as a "prose sonnet" and admitted that the "poetical language" might seem strange to the court but claimed its intent was innocent. Wilde stated that the letters had been obtained by blackmailers who had attempted to extort money from him, but he had refused, suggesting they should take the £60 (equal to £6,800 today) offered, "unusual for a prose piece of that length". He claimed to regard the letters as works of art rather than something of which to be ashamed.

Carson, a fellow Dubliner who had attended Trinity College, Dublin at the same time as Wilde, cross-examined Wilde on how he perceived the moral content of his works. Wilde replied with characteristic wit and flippancy, claiming that works of art are not capable of being moral or immoral but only well or poorly made, and that only "brutes and illiterates", whose views on art "are incalculably stupid", would make such judgements about art. Carson, a leading barrister, diverged from the normal practice of asking closed questions. Carson pressed Wilde on each topic from every angle, squeezing out nuances of meaning from Wilde's answers, removing them from their aesthetic context and portraying Wilde as evasive and decadent. While Wilde won the most laughs from the court, Carson scored the most legal points. To undermine Wilde's credibility, and to justify Queensberry's description of Wilde as a "posing somdomite", Carson drew from the witness an admission of his capacity for "posing", by demonstrating that he had lied about his age on oath. Playing on this, he returned to the topic throughout his cross-examination. Carson also tried to justify Queensberry's characterisation by quoting from Wilde's novel, The Picture of Dorian Gray, referring in particular to a scene in the second chapter, in which Lord Henry Wotton explains his decadent philosophy to Dorian, an "innocent young man", in Carson's words.

Carson then moved to the factual evidence and questioned Wilde about his friendships with younger, lower-class men. Wilde admitted being on a first-name basis and lavishing gifts upon them, but insisted that nothing untoward had occurred and that the men were merely good friends of his. Carson repeatedly pointed out the unusual nature of these relationships and insinuated that the men were prostitutes. Wilde replied that he did not believe in social barriers, and simply enjoyed the society of young men. Then Carson asked Wilde directly whether he had ever kissed a certain servant boy, Wilde responded, "Oh, dear no. He was a particularly plain boy – unfortunately ugly – I pitied him for it." Carson pressed him on the answer, repeatedly asking why the boy's ugliness was relevant. Wilde hesitated, then for the first time became flustered: "You sting me and insult me and try to unnerve me; and at times one says things flippantly when one ought to speak more seriously."

In his opening speech for the defence, Carson announced that he had located several male prostitutes who were to testify that they had had sex with Wilde. On the advice of his lawyers, Wilde dropped the prosecution. Queensberry was found not guilty, as the court declared that his accusation that Wilde was "posing as a Somdomite " was justified, "true in substance and in fact".Under the Libel Act 1843, Queensberry's acquittal rendered Wilde legally liable for the considerable expenses Queensberry had incurred in his defence, which left Wilde bankrupt.

Regina v. Wilde

After Wilde left the court, a warrant for his arrest was applied for on charges of sodomy and gross indecency. Robbie Ross found Wilde at the Cadogan Hotel, Pont Street, Knightsbridge, with Reginald Turner; both men advised Wilde to go at once to Dover and try to get a boat to France; his mother advised him to stay and fight. Wilde, lapsing into inaction, could only say, "The train has gone. It's too late."On 6 April 1895, Wilde was arrested for "gross indecency" under Section 11 of the Criminal Law Amendment Act 1885, a term meaning homosexual acts not amounting to buggery (an offence under a separate statute). At Wilde's instruction, Ross and Wilde's butler forced their way into the bedroom and library of 16 Tite Street, packing some personal effects, manuscripts, and letters. Wilde was then imprisoned on remand at Holloway, where he received daily visits from Douglas.

Events moved quickly and his prosecution opened on 26 April 1895, before Mr Justice Charles. Wilde pleaded not guilty. He had already begged Douglas to leave London for Paris, but Douglas complained bitterly, even wanting to give evidence; he was pressed to go and soon fled to the Hotel du Monde. Fearing persecution, Ross and many others also left the United Kingdom during this time. Under cross examination Wilde was at first hesitant, then spoke eloquently:

> **Charles Gill** (prosecuting): What is "the love that dare not speak its name"?
>
> **Wilde:** "The love that dare not speak its name" in this century is such a great affection of an elder for a younger man as there was between David and Jonathan, such as Plato made the very basis of his philosophy, and such as you find in the sonnets of Michelangelo and Shakespeare. It is that deep spiritual affection that is as pure as it is perfect. It dictates and pervades great works of art, like those of Shakespeare and Michelangelo, and those two letters of mine, such as they are. It is in this century misunderstood, so much misunderstood that it may be described as "the love that dare not speak its name", and on that account of it I am placed where I am now. It is beautiful, it is fine, it is the noblest form of affection. There is nothing unnatural about it. It is intellectual, and it repeatedly exists between an older and a younger man, when the older man has intellect, and the younger man has all the joy, hope and glamour of life before him. That it should be so, the world does not understand. The world mocks at it, and sometimes puts one in the pillory for it.

This response was counter-productive in a legal sense as it only served to reinforce the charges of homosexual behaviour.

The trial ended with the jury unable to reach a verdict. Wilde's counsel, Sir Edward Clarke, was finally able to get a magistrate to allow Wilde and his friends to post bail. The Reverend Stewart Headlam put up most of the £5,000 surety required by the court, having disagreed with Wilde's treatment by the press and the courts. Wilde was freed from Holloway and, shunning attention, went into hiding at the house of Ernest and Ada Leverson, two of his firm friends. Edward Carson approached Frank Lockwood QC, the Solicitor General and asked "Can we not let up on the fellow now?"Lockwood answered that he would like to do so, but feared that the case had become too politicised to be dropped.

The final trial was presided over by Mr Justice Wills. On 25 May 1895 Wilde and Alfred Taylor were convicted of gross indecency and sentenced to two years' hard labour.The judge described the sentence, the maximum allowed, as "totally inadequate for a case such as this", and that the case was "the worst case I have ever tried". Wilde's response "And I? May I say nothing, my Lord?" was drowned out in cries of "Shame" in the courtroom.

Imprisonment

When first I was put into prison some people advised me to try and forget who I was. It was ruinous advice. It is only by realising what I am that I have found comfort of any kind. Now I am advised by others to try on my release to forget that I have ever been in a prison at all. I know that would be equally fatal. It would mean that I would always be haunted by an intolerable sense of disgrace, and that those things that are meant for me as much as for anybody else – the beauty of the sun and moon, the pageant of the seasons, the music of daybreak and the silence of great nights, the rain falling through the leaves, or the dew creeping over the grass and making it silver – would all be tainted for me, and lose their healing power, and their power of communicating joy. To regret one's own experiences is to arrest one's own development. To deny one's own experiences is to put a lie into the lips of one's own life. It is no less than a denial of the soul.

De Profundis

Wilde was incarcerated from 25 May 1895 to 18 May 1897.

He first entered Newgate Prison in London for processing, then was moved to Pentonville Prison, where the "hard labour" to which he had been sentenced consisted of many hours of walking a treadmill and picking oakum (separating the fibres in scraps of old navy ropes), and where prisoners were allowed to read only the Bible and The Pilgrim's Progress.

A few months later he was moved to Wandsworth Prison in London. Inmates there also followed the regimen of "hard labour, hard fare and a hard bed", which wore harshly on Wilde's delicate health. In November he collapsed during chapel from illness and hunger. His right ear drum was ruptured in the fall, an injury that later contributed to his death. He spent two months in the infirmary.

Richard B. Haldane, the Liberal MP and reformer, visited Wilde and had him transferred in November to Reading Gaol, 30 miles (48 km) west of London on 23 November 1895. The transfer itself was the lowest point of his incarceration, as a crowd jeered and spat at him on the railway platform. He spent the remainder of his sentence there, addressed and identified only as "C33" – the occupant of the third cell on the third floor of C ward.

About five months after Wilde arrived at Reading Gaol, Charles Thomas Wooldridge, a trooper in the Royal Horse Guards, was brought to Reading to await his trial for murdering his wife on 29 March 1896; on 17 June Wooldridge was sentenced to death and returned to Reading for his execution, which took place on Tuesday, 7 July 1896 – the first hanging at Reading in 18 years. From Wooldridge's hanging, Wilde later wrote The Ballad of Reading Gaol.

Wilde was not, at first, even allowed paper and pen but Haldane eventually succeeded in allowing access to books and writing materials. Wilde requested, among others: the Bible in French; Italian and German grammars; some Ancient Greek texts, Dante's Divine Comedy, Joris-Karl Huysmans's new French novel about Christian redemption En route, and essays by St Augustine, Cardinal Newman and Walter Pater.

Between January and March 1897 Wilde wrote a 50,000-word letter to Douglas. He was not allowed to send it, but was permitted to take it with him when released from prison. In reflective mode, Wilde coldly examines his career to date, how he had been a colourful agent provocateur in Victorian society, his art, like his paradoxes, seeking to subvert as well as sparkle. His own estimation of himself was: one who "stood in symbolic relations to the art and culture of my age". It was from these heights that his life with Douglas began, and Wilde examines that particularly closely, repudiating him for what Wilde finally sees as his arrogance and vanity: he had not forgotten Douglas' remark, when he was ill, "When you are not on your pedestal you are not interesting." Wilde blamed himself, though, for the ethical degradation of character that he allowed Douglas to bring about in him and took responsibility for his own fall, "I am here for having tried to put your father in prison." The first half concludes with Wilde forgiving Douglas, for his own sake as much as Douglas's. The second half of the letter traces Wilde's spiritual journey of redemption and fulfilment through his prison reading. He realised that his ordeal had filled his soul with the fruit of experience, however bitter it tasted at the time.

> ... I wanted to eat of the fruit of all the trees in the garden of the world ... And so, indeed, I went out, and so I lived. My only mistake was that I confined myself so exclusively to the trees of what seemed to me the sun-lit side of the garden, and shunned the other side for its shadow and its gloom.

Wilde was released from prison on 19 May 1897 and sailed that evening for Dieppe, France. He never returned to the UK.

On his release, he gave the manuscript to Ross, who may or may not have carried out Wilde's instructions to send a copy to Douglas (who later denied having received it). The letter was partially published in 1905 as De Profundis; its complete and correct publication first occurred in 1962 in The Letters of Oscar Wilde.

Decline: 1897–1900

Exile

Though Wilde's health had suffered greatly from the harshness and diet of prison, he had a feeling of spiritual renewal. He immediately wrote to the Society of Jesus requesting a six-month Catholic retreat; when the request was denied, Wilde wept. "I intend to be received into the Catholic Church before long", Wilde told a journalist who asked about his religious intentions.

He spent his last three years impoverished and in exile. He took the name "Sebastian Melmoth", after Saint Sebastian and the titular character of Melmoth the Wanderer (a Gothic novel by Charles Maturin, Wilde's great-uncle).Wilde wrote two long letters to the editor of the Daily Chronicle, describing the brutal conditions of English prisons and advocating penal reform. His discussion of the dismissal of Warder Martin for giving biscuits to an anaemic child prisoner repeated the themes of the corruption and degeneration of punishment that he had earlier outlined in The Soul of Man under Socialism.

Wilde spent mid-1897 with Robert Ross in the seaside village of Berneval-le-Grand in northern France, where he wrote The Ballad of Reading Gaol, narrating the execution of Charles Thomas Wooldridge, who murdered his wife in a rage at her infidelity. It moves from an objective story-telling to symbolic identification with the prisoners. No attempt is made to assess the justice of the laws which convicted them but rather the poem highlights the brutalisation of the punishment that all convicts share. Wilde juxtaposes the executed man and himself with the line "Yet each man kills the thing he loves". He adopted the proletarian ballad form and the author was credited as "C33", Wilde's cell number in Reading Gaol. He suggested that it be published in Reynolds' Magazine, "because it circulates widely among the criminal classes – to which I now belong – for once I will be read by my peers – a new experience for me". It was an immediate roaring commercial success, going through seven editions in less than two years, only after which "[Oscar" was added to the title page, though many in literary circles had known Wilde to be the author. It brought him a small amount of money.

Although Douglas had been the cause of his misfortunes, he and Wilde were reunited in August 1897 at Rouen. This meeting was disapproved of by the friends and families of both men. Constance Wilde was already refusing to meet Wilde or allow him to see their sons, though she sent him money – three pounds a week. During the latter part of 1897, Wilde and Douglas lived together near Naples for a few months until they were separated by their families under the threat of cutting off all funds.

Wilde's final address was at the dingy Hôtel d'Alsace (now known as L'Hôtel), on rue des Beaux-Arts in Saint-Germain-des-Prés, Paris. "This poverty really breaks one's heart: it is so sale , so utterly depressing, so hopeless. Pray do what you can" he wrote to his publisher. He corrected and published An Ideal Husband and The Importance of Being Earnest, the proofs of which, according to Ellmann, show a man "very much in command of himself and of the play" but he refused to write anything else: "I can write, but have lost the joy of writing".

He wandered the boulevards alone and spent what little money he had on alcohol. A series of embarrassing chance encounters with hostile English visitors, or Frenchmen he had known in better days, drowned his spirit. Soon Wilde was sufficiently confined to his hotel to joke, on one of his final trips outside, "My wallpaper and I are fighting a duel to the death. One of us has got to go". On 12 October 1900 he sent a telegram to Ross: "Terribly weak. Please come". His moods fluctuated; Max Beerbohm relates how their mutual friend Reginald 'Reggie' Turner had found Wilde very depressed after a nightmare. "I dreamt that I had died, and was supping with the dead!" "I am sure", Turner replied, "that you must have been the life and soul of the party." Turner was one of the few of the old circle who remained with Wilde to the end and was at his bedside when he died.

Death

By 25 November 1900 Wilde had developed meningitis, then called "cerebral meningitis". Robbie Ross arrived on 29 November, sent for a priest, and Wilde was conditionally baptised into the Catholic Church by Fr Cuthbert Dunne, a Passionist priest from Dublin, Wilde having been baptised in the Church of Ireland and having moreover a recollection of Catholic baptism as a child, a fact later attested to by the minister of the sacrament, Fr Lawrence Fox. Fr Dunne recorded the baptism,

> As the voiture rolled through the dark streets that wintry night, the sad story of Oscar Wilde was in part repeated to me... Robert Ross knelt by the bedside, assisting me as best he could while I administered conditional baptism, and afterwards answering the responses while I

gave Extreme Unction to the prostrate man and recited the prayers for the dying. As the man was in a semi-comatose condition, I did not venture to administer the Holy Viaticum; still I must add that he could be roused and was roused from this state in my presence. When roused, he gave signs of being inwardly conscious... Indeed I was fully satisfied that he understood me when told that I was about to receive him into the Catholic Church and gave him the Last Sacraments... And when I repeated close to his ear the Holy Names, the Acts of Contrition, Faith, Hope and Charity, with acts of humble resignation to the Will of God, he tried all through to say the words after me.

Wilde died of meningitis on 30 November 1900. Different opinions are given as to the cause of the disease: Richard Ellmann claimed it was syphilitic; Merlin Holland, Wilde's grandson, thought this to be a misconception, noting that Wilde's meningitis followed a surgical intervention, perhaps a mastoidectomy; Wilde's physicians, Dr Paul Cleiss and A'Court Tucker, reported that the condition stemmed from an old suppuration of the right ear (from the prison injury, see above) treated for several years (une ancienne suppuration de l'oreille droite d'ailleurs en traitement depuis plusieurs années) and made no allusion to syphilis.

Burial

Wilde was initially buried in the Cimetière de Bagneux outside Paris; in 1909 his remains were disinterred and transferred to Père Lachaise Cemetery, inside the city. His tomb there was designed by Sir Jacob Epstein. It was commissioned by Robert Ross, who asked for a small compartment to be made for his own ashes, which were duly transferred in 1950. The modernist angel depicted as a relief on the tomb was originally complete with male genitalia, which were initially censored by French Authorities with a golden leaf. The genitals have since been vandalised; their current whereabouts are unknown. In 2000, Leon Johnson, a multimedia artist, installed a silver prosthesis to replace them. In 2011, the tomb was cleaned of the many lipstick marks left there by admirers and a glass barrier was installed to prevent further marks or damage.

The epitaph is a verse from The Ballad of Reading Gaol,

And alien tears will fill for him

Pity's long-broken urn,

For his mourners will be outcast men,

And outcasts always mourn.

Posthumous pardon

In 2017, Wilde was among an estimated 50,000 men who were pardoned for homosexual acts that were no longer considered offences under the Policing and Crime Act 2017. The Act is known informally as the Alan Turing law.

Honours

In 2014 Wilde was one of the inaugural honorees in the Rainbow Honor Walk, a walk of fame in San Francisco's Castro neighbourhood noting LGBTQ people who have "made significant contributions in their fields."

Biographies

Wilde's life has been the subject of numerous biographies since his death. The earliest were memoirs by those who knew him: often they are personal or impressionistic accounts which can be good character sketches, but are sometimes factually unreliable. Frank Harris, his friend and editor, wrote a biography, Oscar Wilde: His Life and Confessions (1916); though prone to exaggeration and sometimes factually inaccurate, it offers a good literary portrait of Wilde. Lord Alfred Douglas wrote two books about his relationship with Wilde. Oscar Wilde and Myself (1914), largely ghost-written by T. W. H. Crosland, vindictively reacted to Douglas's discovery that De Profundis was addressed to him and defensively tried to distance him from Wilde's scandalous reputation. Both authors later regretted their work. Later, in Oscar Wilde: A Summing Up (1939) and his Autobiography he was more sympathetic to Wilde. Of Wilde's other close friends, Robert Sherard; Robert Ross, his literary executor; and Charles Ricketts variously published biographies, reminiscences or correspondence. The first more or less objective biography of Wilde came about when Hesketh Pearson wrote Oscar Wilde: His Life and Wit (1946). In 1954 Wilde's son Vyvyan Holland published his memoir Son of Oscar Wilde, which recounts the difficulties Wilde's wife and children faced after his imprisonment. It was revised and updated by Merlin Holland in 1989.

Oscar Wilde, a critical study by Arthur Ransome was published in 1912. The book only briefly mentioned Wilde's life, but subsequently Ransome (and The Times Book Club) were sued for libel by Lord Alfred Douglas. In April 1913 Douglas lost the libel action after a reading of De Profundis refuted his claims.

Richard Ellmann wrote his 1987 biography Oscar Wilde, for which he posthumously won a National (USA) Book Critics Circle Award in 1988and a Pulitzer Prize in 1989. The book was the basis for the 1997 film Wilde, directed by Brian Gilbert and starring Stephen Fry as the title character.

Neil McKenna's 2003 biography, The Secret Life of Oscar Wilde, offers an exploration of Wilde's sexuality. Often speculative in nature, it was widely criticised for its pure conjecture and lack of scholarly rigour. Thomas Wright's Oscar's Books (2008) explores Wilde's reading from his childhood in Dublin to his death in Paris. After tracking down many books that once belonged to Wilde's Tite Street library (dispersed at the time of his trials), Wright was the first to examine Wilde's marginalia.

> Later on, I think everyone will recognise his achievements; his plays and essays will endure. Of course, you may think with others that his personality and conversation were far more wonderful than anything he wrote, so that his written works give only a pale reflection of his power. Perhaps that is so, and of course, it will be impossible to reproduce what is gone forever.

Robert Ross, 23 December 1900

In 2018, Matthew Sturgis' "Oscar: A Life," was published in London. The book incorporates rediscovered letters and other documents and is the most extensively researched biography of Wilde to appear since 1988.

Parisian literati, also produced several biographies and monographs on him. André Gide wrote In Memoriam, Oscar Wilde and Wilde also features in his journals. Thomas Louis, who had earlier translated books on Wilde into French, produced his own L'esprit d'Oscar Wilde in 1920. Modern books include Philippe Jullian's Oscar Wilde, and L'affaire Oscar Wilde, ou, Du danger de laisser la justice mettre le nez dans nos draps (The Oscar Wilde Affair, or, On the Danger of Allowing Justice to put its Nose in our Sheets) by Odon Vallet, a French religious historian. (Source: Wikipedia)

NOTABLE WORKS

ESSAYS

"The Decay of Lying" First published in Nineteenth Century (1889), republished in Intentions (1891).

"Pen, Pencil and Poison" First published in the Fortnightly Review (1889), republished in Intentions (1891).

"The Soul of Man under Socialism" First published in the Fortnightly Review (1891), republished in The Soul of Man (1895), privately printed.

Intentions (1891) Wilde revised his dialogues on aesthetic subjects for publication in this volume, which comprises:

- "The Critic as Artist"
- "The Decay of Lying"
- "Pen, Pencil and Poison"
- "The Truth of Masks"

"Phrases and Philosophies for the Use of the Young" first published in the Oxford student magazine The Chameleon, December 1894)

"A Few Maxims For The Instruction Of The Over-Educated" First published, anonymously, in the 1894 November 17 issue of Saturday Review.

FICTION

Novel

The Picture of Dorian Gray (1890/1891). The first version of "The Picture of Dorian Gray" was published, in a form highly edited by the magazine, as the lead story in the July 1890 edition of Lippincott's Monthly Magazine. Wilde published the longer and revised version in book form in 1891, with an added preface.

Stories

"The Portrait of Mr. W. H." (1889)

The Happy Prince and Other Tales (1888, a collection of fairy tales) consisting of:

- "The Happy Prince"

- "The Nightingale and the Rose"

- "The Selfish Giant"

- "The Devoted Friend"

- "The Remarkable Rocket"

A House of Pomegranates (1891, fairy tales)

Lord Arthur Savile's Crime and Other Stories (1891) Including "The Canterville Ghost" first published in periodical form in 1887.

Complete Short Fiction. Penguin Classics, 2003. Edited with an Introduction and Notes by Ian Small. Contains all works listed above plus Poems in Prose (1894) and one very short 'Elder-tree' (fragment).

POEMS

Ravenna (1878) Winner of the Newdigate Prize.

Poems (1881) Wilde's collection of poetry and first publication.

The Sphinx (1894)

Poems in Prose (1894)

The Ballad of Reading Gaol (1898)

PLAYS

Vera; or, The Nihilists (1880)

The Duchess of Padua (1883)

Lady Windermere's Fan (1892)

A Woman of No Importance (1893)

Salomé (French version) (1893, first performed in Paris 1896)

Salomé: A Tragedy in One Act: Translated from the French of Oscar Wilde by Lord Alfred Douglas, illustrated by Aubrey Beardsley (1894)

An Ideal Husband (1895) (text)

The Importance of Being Earnest (1895) (text)

La Sainte Courtisane and A Florentine Tragedy Fragmentary. First published 1908 in Methuen's Collected Works

(Dates are dates of first performance, which approximate better to the probable date of composition than dates of publication.)

The Importance of Being Earnest and Other Plays. Penguin Classics, 2000. Edited with an Introduction, Commentaries and Notes by Richard Allen Cave. Contains all from above save the first two. Salome is in English.

As an appendix there is one excised scene from The Importance of Being Earnest.

POSTHUMOUS (PREVIOUSLY UNPUBLISHED)

De Profundis (Written 1895-97, in Reading Gaol). Expurgated edition published 1905; suppressed portions 1913, expanded version in The Letters of Oscar Wilde (1962).

The Rise of Historical Criticism (Written while at college) First published in 1905 (Sherwood Press, Hartford, CT) privately printed. Reprinted in Miscellanies, the last volume of the First Collected Edition (1908).

The First Collected Edition (Methuen & Co., 14 volumes) appeared in 1908 and contained many previously unpublished works.

The Second Collected Edition (Methuen & Co., 12 volumes) appeared in installments between 1909–11 and contained several other unpublished works.

The Letters of Oscar Wilde (Written 1868-1900) Published in 1962. Republished as The Complete Letters of Oscar Wilde (2000), with letters discovered since 1962, and new annotations by Merlin Holland.

The Women of Homer (Written 1876, while at college). First published in Oscar Wilde: The Women of Homer (2008) by The Oscar Wilde Society.

The Philosophy of Dress First published in The New-York Tribune (1885), published for the first time in book form in Oscar Wilde On Dress (2013).

MISATTRIBUTED

Teleny, or The Reverse of the Medal (Paris, 1893) has been attributed to Wilde, but its authorship is unclear. One theory is that it was a combined effort by several of Wilde's friends, which he may have edited.

Constance On September 14, 2011, Wilde's grandson Merlin Holland contested Wilde's claimed authorship of this play entitled Constance, scheduled to open that week in the King's Head Theatre. It was not, in fact, "Oscar Wilde's final play," as its producers were claiming. Holland said Wilde did sketch out the play's scenario in 1894, but "never wrote a word" of it, and that "it is dishonest to foist this on the public." The Artistic Director Adam Spreadbury-Maher of the King's Head Theatre and producer of Constance pointed out that Wilde's son, Vyvyan Holland, wrote in 1954, "a significant amount of the dialogue (of Constance) bears the authentic stamp of my father's hand". There is further proof that the developed scenario that Constance was reconstituted from was written by Wilde between 1897 and his death in 1900, rather than the 1894 George Alexander scenario which Merlin Holland quotes.